HELL

"[In Hell] their worm does not die,
and the fire is not quenched.
For everyone will be salted with fire."
(Mark 9:48-49)

HELL

DR. JAEROCK LEE

URIM
BOOKS

HELL by Dr. Jaerock Lee

Published by Urim Books (Representative: Seongkeon Vin)
235-3, Guro-dong 3, Guro-gu, Seoul, Korea
www.urimbooks.com

Previously published in Korean by Urim Books in 2002

First Edition   *1ˢᵗ Printing April 2004*
                       2ⁿᵈ Printing October 2004
Second Edition *1ˢᵗ Printing August 2005*
                       2ⁿᵈ Printing January 2006
Third Edition   *1ˢᵗ Printing August 2009*
                       2ⁿᵈ Printing September 2010

Edited by Dr. Geumsun Vin
Designed by Editorial Bureau of Urim Books
Printed by Yewon Printing Company
For more information contact at urimbook@hotmail.com

Preface

Hoping that this book will serve as the bread of life that leads countless souls to the beautiful Heaven by allowing them to understand the love of God who wants all people to receive salvation...

Today, when people hear about Heaven and Hell, most of them respond negatively, saying, "How can I believe such things in this age of scientific civilization?" "Have you ever been to Heaven and Hell?" or "You know about these things only after you die."

You must know in advance that there is the life after death. It is too late by the time you draw your last breath. After the last breath in this world, you will never have another chance to live the life over. Only God's Judgment, through which you will reap what you sow in this world, awaits you.

Through the Bible, God has already revealed to us the

way of salvation, the existence of Heaven and Hell, and the Judgment that will take place in accordance with the Word of God. He manifested wonderful works of His power through many Old Testament prophets and Jesus.

Even today, God shows you that He is alive and that the Bible is true by manifesting miracles, signs, and other wonderful works of His power recorded in the Bible through His most loyal and faithful servants. Despite abundant evidence of His works, however, there are unbelievers. Thus, God has shown His children Heaven and Hell, and encouraged them to witness to what they have seen all over the world.

The God of love also revealed to me Heaven and Hell in detail and urged me to proclaim the message across the globe as Christ's Second Advent is very near.

When I delivered messages on miserable and revolting scenes in the Lower Grave belonging to Hell, I saw much of my congregation trembling in distress and bursting into tears for souls who have fallen into terrible and cruel punishments in the Lower Grave.

Unsaved souls stay in the Lower Grave only until the Judgment of the Great White Throne takes place. After the Judgment, unsaved souls will fall into either the lake of fire or the lake of burning sulfur. Punishments in the lake of fire or the lake of burning sulfur are much harsher than punishments in the Lower Grave.

I am writing what God has revealed to me through the work of the Holy Spirit based on the Word of God in the Bible. This book can be called a message of sincere love from our God the Father who wants to save as many people as possible from sin by letting them know in advance of the never-ending misery of Hell.

God has given His own Son to die on the cross to save all men. He also wants to prevent even one soul from falling into the wretched Hell. God regards one soul more valuable than the whole world and thus He is extremely delighted and pleased, and celebrates with heavenly hosts and angels when one is saved in faith.

I give all the glory and thanks to God who has led me to publish this book. I hope that you will come to understand the heart of God who does not want to lose even a soul to Hell, and that you will obtain true faith. Furthermore, I urge you to diligently proclaim the gospel to all those souls running toward Hell.

I also give thanks to the Urim Books and its staff including Geumsun Vin, Director of Editorial Bureau. I hope all the readers will realize the fact that there are indeed an eternal life after death and the Judgment, and receive perfect salvation.

Jaerock Lee

Foreword

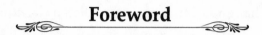

Praying that countless souls may understand the misery of Hell, repent, return from the way of death, and be saved...

The Holy Spirit inspired Dr. Jaerock Lee, Senior Pastor of Manmin Central Church to learn about the life after death and the miserable Hell. We have compiled his messages and today publish *Hell* so that countless people may know about Hell with clarity and accuracy. I give all the glory and thanks to God.

Many people today are curious about life after death, but it is impossible for us to obtain any answers with our limited capacities. This book is a vivid and comprehensive account of Hell, which has been partially revealed to us in the Bible.

Hell also encourages you to understand the love of God who wants all souls to receive salvation and keep alert in faith. *Hell* closes by urging you to lead as many souls as possible to the way of salvation.

God is full of mercy and compassion, and love itself. Today, with the heart of a father waiting for his prodigal son to return, God is earnestly waiting for all lost souls to get rid of sins and receive salvation.

Therefore, I earnestly hope that countless souls around the world will understand and realize that this miserable Hell truly exists, and return to God soon. I also pray in the name of Jesus Christ that all believers in the Lord may keep themselves alert and awake, and lead as many people as they are able to Heaven.

Geumsun Vin
Director of Editorial Bureau

Table of Contents

Chapter 1

Are There Really Heaven and Hell?

"Now the poor man died and was carried away by the angels to Abraham's bosom; and the rich man also died and was buried. In Hades he lifted up his eyes, being in torment, and saw Abraham far away and Lazarus in his bosom. And he cried out and said, 'Father Abraham, have mercy on me, and send Lazarus so that he may dip the tip of his finger in water and cool off my tongue, for I am in agony in this flame.' But Abraham said, 'Child, remember that during your life you received your good things, and likewise Lazarus bad things; but now he is being comforted here, and you are in agony. And besides all this, between us and you there is a great chasm fixed, so that those who wish to come over from here to you will not be able, and that none may cross over from there to us.' And he said, 'Then I beg you, father, that you send him to my father's house for I have five brothers in order that he may warn them, so that they will not also come to this place of torment.' But Abraham said, 'They have Moses and the Prophets; let them hear them.' But he said, 'No, father Abraham, but if someone goes to them from the dead, they will repent!' But he said to him, 'If they do not listen to Moses and the Prophets, they will not be persuaded even if someone rises from the dead.'"

- Luke 16: 22-31

Most people around us are afraid of death and live in fear and anxiety of losing their lives. Nevertheless, they do not seek God because they do not believe in the life after death. Moreover, many people who profess their faith in Christ also seem to be failing to live in faith. Due to foolishness, people doubt and do not believe in the life after death, even though God has already revealed to us about the life after death, Heaven, and Hell in the Bible.

The life after death is an invisible spiritual world. Thus, people cannot grasp it unless God allows them to know. As written in the Bible repeatedly, Heaven and Hell surely exist. That is why God shows Heaven and Hell to many people all around the world and lets them proclaim them to all corners of the earth.

"Heaven and Hell surely exist."

"Heaven is a beautiful and fascinating place while Hell is a dreary and wretched place beyond your imagination. I strongly urge you to believe in the existence of the life after death."

"It is up to you whether you will go to Heaven or Hell. In order not to fall into Hell, you should repent all your sins immediately and accept Jesus Christ."

"Surely Hell exists. It is where people suffer from fire forever and ever. It is also true that Heaven exists. Heaven can be your permanent home."

The God of love has explained to me about Heaven since May 1984. He has also begun to explain Hell in detail since

March 2000. He asked me to spread what I had learned about Heaven and Hell all over the world so that not even one will be punished in the lake of fire or in the lake of burning sulfur.

God once showed me a soul who was suffering and lamenting with remorse in the Lower Grave, where all those destined to Hell await in agony. The soul refused to accept the Lord despite many opportunities to hear the gospel and eventually fell into Hell after death. The following is his confession:

I count the days.
I count, count, and count but they are endless.
I should have tried to accept Jesus Christ
when they told me about Him.
What shall I do now?

It is utterly useless even if I remorse now.
I do not know what to do now.
I want to escape from this suffering
but I do not know what to do.

I count one day, two days, and three days.
But even if I count days in this way,
I now know it is useless.
My heart is tearing apart.
What shall I do? What shall I do?
How can I be free from this great pain?
What shall I do, oh, my poor soul?
How can I endure it?

Heaven and Hell Surely Exist

Hebrews 9:27 writes that *"And inasmuch as it is appointed for men to die once and after this comes judgment."* All men and women are destined to die and after they take their last breath, they enter either Heaven or Hell after the judgment.

God wants everyone to enter Heaven because He is love. God prepared Jesus Christ before time began and opened the door for salvation of human beings when the time was ripe. God does not want a single soul to fall into Hell.

Romans 5:7-8 proclaims that *"For one will hardly die for a righteous man; though perhaps for the good man someone would dare even to die. But God demonstrates His own love toward us, in that while we were yet sinners, Christ died for us."* Indeed, God demonstrated His love for us by giving His one and only Son unsparingly.

The door of salvation is widely open so that any one accepting Jesus Christ as his or her personal Savior will be saved and enter Heaven. However, most people have no interest in Heaven and Hell even if they hear about them. Furthermore, some of them even persecute people who proclaim the gospel.

The saddest fact is that people who claim to believe in God still love the world and commit sins because they actually have no hope for Heaven and no fear of Hell.

Through the testimonies of witnesses and the Bible

Heaven and Hell are in the spiritual world that truly exists. The Bible mentions many times the existence of Heaven and Hell. Those who have been to Heaven or Hell also witness to them. For example, in the Bible, God tells us how miserable Hell is so that we may obtain an everlasting life in Heaven instead of falling into Hell after death.

If your hand causes you to stumble, cut it off; it is better for you to enter life crippled, than, having your two hands, to go into Hell, into the unquenchable fire, [where their worm does not die, and the fire is not quenched.] If your foot causes you to stumble, cut it off; it is better for you to enter life lame, than, having your two feet, to be cast into Hell, [where their worm does not die, and the fire is not quenched.] If your eye causes you to stumble, throw it out; it is better for you to enter the kingdom of God with one eye, than, having two eyes, to be cast into Hell, where their worm does not die, and the fire is not quenched. For everyone will be salted with fire (Mark 9:43-49).

Those who have been to Hell witness to the same the Bible proclaims. In Hell, *"their worm does not die, and the fire is not quenched. For everyone will be salted with fire."*

It is clear as crystal that there are Heaven and Hell after death as written in the Bible. Therefore, you ought to enter Heaven by living according to the Word of God, believing in the existence of Heaven and Hell in your mind.

You should not lament with remorse as the soul mentioned above suffering without an end in the Lower Grave because he refused to accept the Lord despite many opportunities to hear about the gospel.

In John 14:11-12, Jesus tells us, *"Believe Me that I am in the Father and the Father is in Me; otherwise believe because of the works themselves. Truly, truly, I say to you, he who believes in*

Me, the works that I do, he will do also; and greater works than these he will do; because I go to the Father."

You can recognize a certain person to be a man of God when powerful works beyond human capability accompany him, and you can also confirm that his message is in accordance with the true Word of God.

I spread Jesus Christ, performing work of the power of the living God while I hold crusades all over the world. When I pray in the name of Jesus Christ, countless people believe and receive salvation because the amazing work of power takes place: the blind come to see, the mute speak, the lame stand up, the dying revive, and so forth.

In this way, God has manifested His powerful work through me. He also explains Heaven and Hell in detail and permits me to proclaim them all over the world so that as many people as possible may be saved.

Today, many people are curious about the life after death – the spiritual world – but it is impossible to know about the spiritual world clearly only with human efforts. You can learn about it partly through the Bible. However, you can find it ever so clearly only when God explains it while you are fully inspired by the Holy Spirit who searches all things, even the deep things about God (1 Corinthians 2:10).

I hope that you will fully believe my description of Hell based on verses from the Bible because God Himself explained it to me while I was wholly inspired by the Spirit.

Why proclaim the Judgment of God and punishment in Hell

When I deliver messages on Hell, those who have faith will be filled with the Holy Spirit and listen to them without any fear. However, there are those who become stiff-faced with tension and their usual affirmative response such as "Amen" or "Yes" gradually fades away during the sermon. At worst, people with weak faith stop attending worship services or even leave the church in fear, instead of reaffirming their faith in hope of entering Heaven.

Nevertheless, I must explain Hell because I know the heart of God. God is so anxious of people running toward Hell, still living in darkness, and compromising with the worldly way of life although some of them profess their belief in Jesus Christ.

Therefore, I am going to explain Hell in detail so that the children of God may dwell in the light, forsaking the darkness. God wants His children to repent and enter Heaven even though they may be in fear and feel uncomfortable when they hear about God's Judgment and the punishment in Hell.

The Parable of the Rich Man and the Beggar Lazarus

In Luke 16:19-31, both the rich man and the beggar Lazarus went to the Grave after death. Situations and conditions of places each man was to reside thenceforth were drastically different.

The rich man was in great torment with fire while Lazarus

was in Abraham's side over a great chasm far away. Why?

In Old Testament times, the judgment of God was carried out according to the Law of Moses. On the one hand, the rich man received the punishment of fire because he had not believed in God, although he lived in great luxury in this world. On the other hand, the beggar Lazarus could enjoy the everlasting rest because he had believed in God although he was covered with sores, and longed to eat what fell from the rich man's table.

The life after death determined by the Judgment of God

In the Old Testament, we find our forefathers of faith including Jacob and Job stating that they would go down to the Grave after they died (Genesis 37:35; Job 7:9). Korah and all his men who had risen up against Moses went down into the Grave alive, with the anger of God (Numbers 16:33).

The Old Testament also mentions "Sheol" and "Hades." The Grave is the English Word for both "Sheol" and "Hades." And the Grave is divided into two parts: the Upper Grave belonging to Heaven and the Lower Grave (Hades) belonging to Hell.

Thus, you know that forefathers of faith such as Jacob and Job and the beggar Lazarus went to the Upper Grave belonging to Heaven while Korah and the rich man went to Hades belonging to Hell.

Likewise, there is surely a life after death and all men and women are destined to go to Heaven or Hell according to the Judgment of God. I strongly urge you to believe in God so that you will be saved from going to Hell.

The Structure of Heaven and Hell

The Bible uses various names in mentioning Heaven or Hell. In fact, you recognize that Heaven and Hell are not at the same place.

In other words, Heaven is referred to as "the Upper Grave," "Paradise," or "New Jerusalem." This is because Heaven, the residence of the saved soul, is categorized and divided into many different places.

As I already explained in the messages on *"The Measure of Faith"* and *"Heaven I & II,"* you may live closer to the Throne of God in New Jerusalem to the extent you recover the lost image of God the Father. Alternatively, you may enter the Third Kingdom of Heaven, the Second Kingdom of Heaven, or the First Kingdom of Heaven according to the measure of your faith. Those who are barely saved may enter Paradise.

The residence of unsaved souls or evil spirits is also referred to as "the Lower Grave (Hades)," "the lake of fire," "the lake of burning sulfur," or "the Abyss (the bottomless pit)." Just as Heaven is divided into many places, Hell is also divided into many places because each soul's residence differs from that of one another according to the measure of his evil deeds in this world.

The structure of Heaven and Hell

Imagine a shape of a diamond ($\Diamond$) to better understand the structure of Heaven and Hell. If the shape is cut in half, there are a triangle ($\triangle$) and an upside-down triangle ($\triangledown$). Let us suppose that the upper triangle represents Heaven and the upside-down triangle represents Hell.

The highest part of the upper triangle corresponds to New Jerusalem while the lowest part of it to the Upper Grave. In other words, above the Upper Grave are Paradise, the First Kingdom of Heaven, the Second Kingdom, the Third Kingdom, and New Jerusalem. However, you should not think of different Kingdoms like first, second or third floors of a building in this world. In the spiritual realm, it is impossible to draw a line to separate land as you do here in this world and to tell the shape of it. I only explain it in this way to let people of flesh understand Heaven and Hell more clearly.

In the upper triangle, the apex corresponds to New Jerusalem while the lowest part of it to the Upper Grave. In other words, the higher you go up the triangle, the better Kingdom of Heaven you will find.

In the other figure, the upside-down triangle, the highest and broadest part corresponds to the Lower Grave. The closer you get to the bottom, the deeper part of the Hell you approach; the Lower Grave, the lake with fire, the lake with brimstone, and the Abyss. The Abyss mentioned in the Books of Luke and Revelation refers to the deepest part of Hell. In the upper triangle, the area becomes smaller as you go up from the bottom to the top – from Paradise to New Jerusalem. This shape shows you that the number of people entering New Jerusalem is relatively small compared to the number of people entering Paradise, the First or Second Kingdom of Heaven. It is because only those who accomplish holiness and perfection through sanctification of their hearts, following the heart of God the Father, may enter New Jerusalem.

As you can see in the upside-down triangle, comparatively fewer people go to the deeper part of Hell because only those whose conscience have been branded and who have committed the worst evil are thrown into that place. A greater number of people who commit relatively light sins go to the upper, broader part of Hell.

Thus, Heaven and Hell can be imagined to have a shape of a diamond. However, you should not conclude that Heaven is in a shape of a triangle or Hell is in a shape of an upside-down triangle.

A great chasm between Heaven and Hell

There is a great chasm between the upper triangle – Heaven – and the upside-down triangle – Hell. Heaven and Hell are not adjacent to each other but are distant beyond measure.

God has set a boundary so clearly in this way so that souls in Heaven and Hell could not travel back and forth between Heaven and Hell. Only in a very special case granted by God, is it possible to see and talk to each other the way the rich man and Abraham did.

Between the two symmetrical triangles, there is a great

chasm. People cannot come and go from Heaven to Hell, and vice versa. Nevertheless, if God permits, people in Heaven and Hell can see, hear, and talk to each other in spirit regardless of the distance.

Perhaps you can understand this easily if you remember how we are able to talk to people on the other side of the earth on telephone or even talk face to face on screens via satellites due to the rapid advancement and development of science and technology.

Even though there is a great chasm between Heaven and Hell, the rich man could see Lazarus resting in Abraham's side and talk to Abraham in spirit with God's permission.

The Upper Grave and Paradise

To be accurate, the Upper Grave is not a part of Heaven but can be regarded as belonging to Heaven while the Lower Grave is a part of Hell. The role of the Upper Grave from Old to New Testament times has been transformed.

The Upper Grave in Old Testament times

In Old Testament times, saved souls were waiting in the Upper Grave. Abraham, the forefather of faith, took charge of the Upper Grave and this is why the Bible mentions that Lazarus was in Abraham's side.

However, since the resurrection and ascension of the Lord Jesus Christ, saved souls are not in Abraham's side anymore but are transferred to Paradise and are in the Lord's side. This is why in Luke 23:43, Jesus said, *"Truly I say to you, today you shall be with Me in Paradise"* to one of the robbers who repented and received Jesus as his Savior while Jesus was hung on the cross.

Did Jesus immediately go to Paradise after His crucifixion? 1 Peter 3:18-19 tells us that *"For Christ also died for sins once for all, the just for the unjust, so that He might bring us to God, having been put to death in the flesh, but made alive in the spirit; in which also He went and made proclamation to the spirits now in prison."* From this verse, you can see that Jesus preached the gospel to all would-be-saved souls waiting in the Upper Grave. I will discuss this in detail in chapter 2.

Jesus, who had preached the gospel for three days in the Upper Grave, brought souls who would be saved to Paradise when he resurrected and ascended into Heaven. Today, Jesus is preparing a place for us in Heaven as He said, *"I go to prepare a place for you"* (John 14:2).

Paradise in New Testament times

Saved souls are no longer in the Upper Grave after Jesus widely opened the door of salvation. They reside in the outskirts of Paradise, the Waiting Place to Heaven until the end of the human cultivation. And then after the Judgment of the Great White Throne, each of them will enter his own place in Heaven according to the measure of individual faith and will live there forever and ever.

All saved souls are waiting in Paradise in New Testament times. Some people may wonder if it is possible for so many people to live in Paradise because countless people have been born since Adam. "Pastor Lee! How is it possible for so many people to live in Paradise? I'm afraid that it may not be big enough for all the people to live together even if it is spacious."

The solar system to which the earth belongs is a mere speck compared to a galactic system. Can you imagine how big the galactic system is? However, a galactic system is a mere speck compared to the whole universe. Can you then imagine how spacious the whole universe is?

In addition, the enormous universe in which we live is only one of countless universes, and the vastness of the entire universe is far beyond our imagination. Thus, if it is impossible for you to fathom the vastness of the physical universes, how can you possibly grasp the vastness of Heaven in the spiritual realm?

Paradise itself is very spacious beyond imagination. It is immeasurably distant from the nearest place to the First Kingdom to the rim of Paradise. Can you now imagine how vast Paradise itself is?

Souls gain spiritual knowledge in Paradise

Although in Paradise is a waiting place en route to Heaven, it is not a narrow or boring place. It is so beautiful that it could not be compared to the most stunning scenery of this world.

Waiting souls in Paradise gain spiritual knowledge from some of the prophets. They learn about God and Heaven, spiritual law, and other necessary spiritual knowledge. There is no limit to spiritual knowledge. Studying there is completely different from that in this world. It is not difficult or boring. The more they learn the more grace and joy they receive.

Those who are pure and gentle in heart can gain a great deal of spiritual knowledge through communication with God even in this world. You can also understand many things by the inspiration of the Holy Spirit when you see things with your spiritual eyes. You can experience the spiritual power of God even in this world because you can understand spiritual laws on faith and God's answer to your prayer to the extent that you circumcise your heart.

How happy and fully pleased are you when you learn spiritual things and experience them in this world? Imagine how happier and more joyous you will be when you gain deeper spiritual knowledge in Paradise belonging to Heaven.

Where, then, do those prophets live? Do they live in Paradise? No. Souls qualified to enter New Jerusalem are not waiting in Paradise but in New Jerusalem, helping God with His works there.

Abraham had taken care of the Upper Grave before Jesus was crucified. However, after Jesus' resurrection and ascension, Abraham went to New Jerusalem because he had finished his duty in the Upper Grave. Then, where were Moses and Elijah while Abraham was in the Upper Grave? They were not in Paradise but were already in New Jerusalem because they had been qualified to enter New Jerusalem (Matthew 17:1-3).

The Upper Grave in New Testament times

You might see a movie in which a man's soul resembling his own physical body is separated from his body after death and follows either angels from Heaven or messengers from Hell. In fact, a saved soul is led into Heaven by two angels with white robes after his soul is separated from his body the moment he dies. One who knows or learns this will not be shocked even if his soul is separated from his body when he dies. One who does not know this at all, however, is shocked to see another person exactly looking like himself, separated from his body.

A soul separated from the physical body will feel very strange and weird at first. Its state is very different from the previous one because it now experiences enormous changes, having lived in the three-dimensional but now in the four-dimensional world.

The separated soul does not feel weight of the body and may be tempted to buzz around because the body feels very light. This is why it requires some time to learn about basic things for adjustment to the spiritual world. Therefore, saved souls in New Testament times stay tentatively and adjust to the spiritual world in the Upper Grave before entering Paradise.

The Lower Grave, a Waiting Place En Route to Hell

The uppermost part of Hell is the Lower Grave. As one goes down lower within Hell, there are the lake of fire, the lake of burning sulfur, and the Abyss, the deepest part of Hell. Unsaved souls since the beginning of time are not yet in Hell but still in the Lower Grave.

Many people claim to have been to Hell. I can say that they actually saw tormenting scenes in the Lower Grave. It is because the unsaved souls are confined in different parts of the Lower Grave according to the severity of their sins and evil and eventually, they will be cast into the lake of fire or the lake of burning sulfur after the Judgment of the Great White Throne.

Sufferings of the unsaved souls in the Lower Grave

In Luke 16:24, suffering inflicted upon the unsaved rich man in the Lower Grave is described well. In his agony, the rich man asked for a drop of water, saying, *"Father Abraham, have mercy on me, and send Lazarus so that he may dip the tip of his finger in water and cool off my tongue, for I am in agony in this flame."*

How can the souls not be terrified and tremble in bloodcurdling fear since they are constantly tormented in the midst of other people's cries in agony in the razing fire without even a hope of death in Hell, where worm does not die, and the fire is not quenched?

Brutal messengers of hell torment the souls in the pitch-black darkness, the Lower Grave. The whole place is surrounded by bloodiness and terrible odor from decaying corpses, so it is very difficult even to breathe. However, punishment in Hell is not comparable to that of the Lower Grave.

From chapter 3 on, I will discuss in detail with specific examples how terrifying a place the Lower Grave is and what kind of unbearable punishments are inflicted in the lake of fire and the lake of burning sulfur.

The unsaved souls are so remorseful in the Lower Grave

In Luke 16:27-30, the rich man did not believe in the existence of Hell but he came to know of his foolishness and felt remorse in the fire after his death. The rich man begged Abraham to send Lazarus to his brothers so that they might not come to Hell.

"Then I beg you, father, that you send him to my father's house for I have five brothers in order that he may warn them, so that they will not also come to this place of torment." But Abraham said, "They have Moses and the Prophets; let them hear them." But he said, "No, father Abraham, but if someone goes to them from the dead, they will repent!"

What would the rich man say to his brothers if he were given a chance to talk to them in person? He would surely tell them, "I absolutely know that there is Hell. Please, be sure to live according to the Word of God and not to come to Hell because Hell is a hair-raising and terrible place."

Even in an endless agonizing pain and suffering, the rich man wanted earnestly to save his brothers from coming to Hell, and there is no doubt that he had a relatively good heart. Then, how about people today?

Once God showed me a married couple being tormented in Hell because they had forsaken God and left the church. In Hell, they blamed, cursed, hated each other, and even wanted more pain to fall upon the other.

The rich man wanted his brothers to be saved because he was somewhat good in heart. Yet, you should remember that the rich man was nevertheless thrown into Hell. You must also remember that you cannot gain salvation just by saying, "I believe."

Man is destined to die and will go to either Heaven or Hell after death. Therefore, you should not be foolish but become a true believer.

A wise man prepares himself for the life after death

Wise people truly prepare themselves for the life after death while most people work so arduously to gain and build honor, power, wealth, prosperity, and longevity in this world.

Wise people store up their wealth in Heaven in accordance with the Word of God because they know all too well they are not able to take anything to their graves.

You may have heard some testimonies of those who could not find their own houses in Heaven when they visited there although they had supposedly believed in God and led lives in Christ. You can have a big and beautiful house in Heaven if you diligently store up your wealth in Heaven while you live as God's precious child in this world!

You are truly blessed and wise because you struggle to have and maintain a confident faith to enter the beautiful Heaven and because you diligently store your prize in Heaven in faith, preparing yourself as a bride of the Lord who is to return very soon.

Once a man dies, he cannot live his life over again. Thus, please have faith and know that there are Heaven and Hell. In addition, knowing that unsaved souls are in great torment in Hell, you should proclaim Heaven and Hell to everyone you come across in this life. Imagine how pleased God will be with you!

Those who proclaim the love of God, who wants to lead all people to the way of salvation, will be blessed in this life and will shine like the sun in Heaven as well.

I hope that you will believe in the living God who judges and rewards you, and try to become a true child of God. I pray in the name of the Lord that you will lead as many people as possible back to God and salvation, and be much delighted by God.

Chapter 2

The Way of Salvation for Those Who Never Heard the Gospel

God proved His love for us by giving His one and only Son Jesus Christ to be crucified for the salvation of all men.

Parents love their little children but they want their children to become mature enough to understand their heart and share their joy and pain together.

Likewise, God wants all human beings to be saved. Furthermore, God wants His children to become mature enough in faith to know the heart of God the Father and share deep love with Him. This is why the apostle Paul writes in 1 Timothy 2:4 that God wants all men to be saved and to come to the knowledge of the truth.

You should know that God shows Hell and the spiritual world in detail because God in His love wants all men to receive salvation and become fully mature in faith.

In this chapter, I will explain in detail whether it is possible for those who have died without knowing Jesus Christ to be saved.

Judgment of Conscience

Many people who do not believe in God acknowledge at

least the existence of Heaven and Hell, but they cannot enter Heaven simply because they acknowledge Heaven and Hell.

As Jesus tells us in John 14:6, *"I am the way, and the truth, and the life; no one comes to the Father but through Me,"* you can be saved and enter Heaven only through Jesus Christ.

How, then, can you be saved? The apostle Paul in Romans 10:9-10 shows us a way to concrete salvation:

> *If you confess with your mouth Jesus as Lord, and believe in your heart that God raised Him from the dead, you will be saved; for with the heart a person believes, resulting in righteousness, and with the mouth he confesses, resulting in salvation.*

Let us suppose there are some people who do not know Jesus Christ. As a result, they do not confess, "Jesus is the Lord." Nor do they believe in Jesus Christ with their heart. Then is it true that all of them cannot be saved?

A great deal of people lived before Jesus' coming to the earth. Even in New Testament times, there were people who died without ever hearing the gospel. Can those people be saved?

What would be the destiny of some people who died so early that they were never mature or wise enough to recognize faith? What about unborn children who died from abortion or miscarriage? Do they have to go to Hell unconditionally because they did not believe in Jesus Christ? No, they do not.

The God of love opens the door of salvation for everyone in His justice through the "judgment of conscience."

Those who sought god and lived with good conscience

Romans 1:20 proclaims that *"For since the creation of the world His invisible attributes, His eternal power and divine nature, have been clearly seen, being understood through what has been made, so that they are without excuse."* This is why people with good hearts believe the existence of god by seeing what has been made.

Ecclesiastes 3:11 tells us that God has set eternity in the hearts of men. So good people seek god by nature and vaguely believe in the life after death. Good people fear the heavens and try to lead good and righteous lives even though they may have never heard the gospel. Therefore, they live according to the will of their gods to a certain degree. If they had only heard the gospel, they would have surely accepted the Lord and entered Heaven.

For this very reason, God allowed good souls to stay in the Upper Grave as a way of leading them to Heaven until Jesus died on the cross. After the crucifixion of Jesus, God led them to salvation through the blood of Jesus by letting them hear the gospel.

Hearing the gospel in the Upper Grave

The Bible tells us that Jesus proclaimed the gospel in the Upper Grave after He died on the cross.

As 1 Peter 3:18-19 remarks, *"For Christ also died for sins once for all, the just for the unjust, so that He might bring us to God, having been put to death in the flesh, but made alive in the spirit; in which also He went and made proclamation to the spirits now in prison,"* Jesus proclaimed the gospel to the souls in the Upper Grave so that they could be saved through His blood as well.

23

Upon hearing the gospel, people who had not heard it in their lifetime finally received a chance to know who Jesus Christ was and were saved.

God has given no other name except Jesus Christ to lead man to salvation (Acts 4:12). Even during New Testament times, those who had no opportunity to hear the gospel are saved through the judgment of conscience. They stay in the Upper Grave for three days to hear the gospel and then enter Heaven.

People with filthy conscience never seek God and live in sin, indulging in their own passion. They would not believe in the gospel even if they heard it. After death, they will be sent to the Lower Grave to live in punishment and eventually fall into Hell after the Judgment of the Great White Throne.

The judgment of conscience

It is impossible for one to judge someone else's conscience accurately because a mere man cannot read other people's hearts accurately. Yet, the almighty God can discern everyone's heart and make fair judgments.

Romans 2:14-15 explains the judgment of conscience. Good people know what is good or evil because their consciences allow them to know the requirements of the Law.

For when Gentiles who do not have the Law do instinctively the things of the Law, these, not having the Law, are a law to themselves, in that they show the work of the Law written in their hearts, their conscience bearing witness and their thoughts alternately accusing or else defending them.

Thus, good people do not follow the way of evil but follow

the way of good in their life. Consequently, according to the judgment of conscience, they stay in the Upper Grave for three days, during which they hear the gospel and are saved.

You can name Admiral Soonshin Lee* as exemplar who lived in goodness by his good conscience (*Editor's Note: Admiral Lee was the supreme commander of the navy forces for the Chosun Dynasty in Korea during the sixteenth century). Admiral Lee lived in truth even though he did not know Jesus Christ. He was always loyal to his king, his country, and the people he was protecting. He was good and faithful to his parents and loved his brothers. He never put his own interest above that of others, and never sought honor, authority, or riches. He only served and sacrificed himself for his neighbors and the people.

You cannot find out any trace of evil in him. Admiral Lee was exiled without any complaints or intention to avenge his enemy when he was wrongfully accused. He did not grumble at the king even when the king, who had banished him to exile, ordered him to fight on a battlefield. Instead, he thanked the king with all his heart, set troops in good order again, and fought in battles at the risk of his own life. Furthermore, he spared time to pray to his god on his knees because he recognized the existence of one. For what reasons would God not lead him to Heaven?

Those who are excluded from the judgment of conscience

Are the people who heard the gospel but did not believe in God can be subject to the judgment of conscience?

Your family members could not be subjected to the

judgment of conscience if they did not accept the gospel even after hearing it from you. It is fair for them not to be saved if they rejected the gospel although they had many opportunities to hear it.

Nevertheless, you should proclaim the good news diligently because even if people were wicked enough to go to Hell, you would be allowing them to have more opportunities to receive salvation through your work.

Every child of God is a debtor in the gospel and has an obligation to spread it. God will question you on the Day of Judgment if you have never proclaimed the gospel to your family, including your parents, siblings, and your relatives, and so forth. "Why did you not evangelize to your parents and brothers?" "Why did you not evangelize to your children?" "Why did you not evangelize to your friends?" and so forth.

Therefore, you ought to spread the good news to people day in and day out if you really understand the love of God who even sacrificed His one and only Son, and if you really know the love of the Lord who died on the cross for us.

Saving souls is the very way to quench the thirst of the Lord who cried on the cross, "I am thirsty," and to repay the price of blood of the Lord.

Unborn Babies from Abortion or Miscarriage

What is the fate of unborn babies who die from miscarriage before they are born? After physical death, a human being's spirit is destined to go to either Heaven or Hell because a human being's spirit, even if it is so young, cannot be destroyed.

Spirit given five months after conception

When is a spirit given to a fetus? A spirit is not given to the fetus until the sixth month of the pregnancy.

According to medical science, after five months from conception, a fetus develops hearing organs, eyes, and eyelids. Cerebral lobes that activate the function of cerebrum are also formed five to six months after the conception.

When the fetus is six months old, a spirit is given to it and it has virtually the form of a human being. The fetus does not go to Hell or Heaven when it is miscarried before the spirit is given to it because a fetus without a spirit is as good as an animal.

Ecclesiastes 3:21 says, *"Who knows that the breath of man ascends upward and the breath of the beast descends downward to the earth?"* "The breath of man" here indicates what is combined with man's spirit that was given by God and leads man to search for God and his soul that causes him to think and obey the Word of God, while "the breath of the beast" just refers to the soul, namely the system that causes it to think and act.

A particular animal becomes extinct when it dies because it has only a soul but not a spirit. A fetus of less than five months into the pregnancy does not have a spirit. Thus, if it dies, it will extinguish the way an animal does.

Abortion is as heavy a sin as murder

Then, is it not a sin to abort a fetus less than five months old since it has no spirit in it? You should not commit a sin of aborting a fetus, regardless of the time when a spirit is given to the fetus, remembering that God alone governs human life.

In Psalm 139:15-16, the Psalmist wrote, *"My frame was not hidden from You, when I was made in secret, and skillfully wrought in the depths of the earth; Your eyes have seen my unformed substance; and in Your book were all written the days that were ordained for me, when as yet there was not one of them."*

The God of love knew each one of you before you were formed in your mother's womb and had wonderful ideas and plans for you to the extent to write them in His book. This is why a human being, a mere creature of God, cannot control the life of a fetus, even if it is less than five months old.

Aborting a fetus is the same as committing a murder because you infringe on the authority of God who governs life, death, blessing, and cursing. Furthermore, how can you dare to insist it is an insignificant sin when you kill your own son or daughter?

Retributions of sin and trials ensue

Under any circumstances and no matter how difficult, should you never violate the sovereignty of God on human life. Moreover, it is not proper to abort your child in the pursuit of pleasure. You must realize that you will reap what you sow, and you will pay for what you have done.

It is more serious if you abort a fetus after six months or more into the pregnancy. It is the same as murdering a grownup because a spirit has already been given to it.

Abortion creates a big wall of sin between you and God. As a result, you are inflicted with pains stemming from various trials and troubles. Gradually, you are estranged from God due to the wall of sin if you do not resolve the problem of sin, and eventually you may have gone too far to be able to return.

Even those who do not believe in God would be punished and all kinds of trials and troubles will be brought upon them if they commit feticide since it is a murder. Trials and troubles always accompany them since God cannot protect them and turns His face from them if they do not tear down the wall of sin.

Repent your sins thoroughly and tear down the wall of sin

God gave His commands not to condemn human beings but to reveal His will, lead them to repentance, and save them.

God also allows you to understand these things relevant to abortion so that you may not commit this sin and can destroy the wall of sin by repenting your sins committed in the past.

If you aborted your child in the past, be sure to repent thoroughly and tear down the wall of sin by giving peace offering. Then, trials and trouble will disappear as God will no longer remember your sins.

The severity of sin is different case by case when you abort your child. For example, if you aborted your child because you were impregnated from rape, your sin is relatively light. If a married couple aborted their unwanted child, their sin is more severe.

If you do not want a child for a variety of reasons, you should commit your child in your womb to God in prayer. In such a case, you should give birth to your child if God does not work in accordance with your prayer.

Most aborted children are saved but there are exceptions

Six months after conception, a fetus, even though it is given a spirit, cannot reasonably think, understand, or believe something in its own will. Thus, God saves most of the fetuses who die in this period regardless of their faith or that of their parents.

Notice how I said "most" – not "all" – of the fetuses because in rare instances, a fetus may not be saved.

A fetus can inherit wicked nature from the moment of conception if its parents or forefathers contended greatly against God and piled up evil upon evil. In this case, the fetus cannot be saved.

For instance, it can be a child of a magician or a child of wicked parents who cursed and wished only ill for other people such as Hee-bin Jang* in Korean history (*Editor's Note: Lady Jang was a concubine of King Sook-jong in the late seventeenth century, who, out of jealousy, cursed the Queen). She cursed her rival by piercing a portrait of the rival with arrows in extreme jealousy. Children of such wicked parents cannot be saved because they inherit their parents' evil nature.

There are also extremely wicked people among those who claim to believe. Such people oppose, misjudge, condemn, and hinder the work of the Holy Spirit. In jealousy, they also try to kill one who glorifies the name of God. If children of such parents were miscarried, they cannot be saved.

With the exception of such rare cases, most of unborn children are saved. However, they cannot enter Heaven, even Paradise since they were not cultivated on this earth at all. They live in the Upper Grave even after the Judgment of the Great White Throne takes place.

Eternal Place for saved unborn babies

Fetuses aborted six months or after into the pregnancy in

the Upper Grave are just like a blank sheet of paper since they are not cultivated on earth. Therefore, they would stay in the Upper Grave and will put on body suitable for their souls at the time of resurrection.

They put on body that will change and grow unlike other saved people who put on spiritual and everlasting body. Therefore, even though they are in the state and shape of children at first, they would grow until they reach a proper stage.

These children, even after they grow up, remain in the Upper Grave, filling their souls with the knowledge of truth. You can understand this easily if you think about Adam's initial state in the Garden of Eden and his learning process.

Adam was composed of spirit, soul, and body when he was created as a living being. However, his body was different from spiritual, resurrected body and his soul was ignorant like that of a newborn baby. Therefore, God Himself gave Adam spiritual knowledge, walking with him for quite a long period.

You should know that Adam in the Garden of Eden was created without any evil in him but souls in the Upper Grave are not as good as Adam was, because they have already inherited sinful nature from their parents who had experienced the human cultivation for generations.

Ever since the Fall of Adam, all of his descendants thereafter have inherited the original sin from their parents.

Children from Birth to the Age of Five

How can children up to five years of age, who cannot tell what is good or bad and do not recognize faith yet, be saved?

Salvation of children of this age is dependant upon the faith of their parents – especially, their mothers.

A child can receive salvation if parents of the child have the kind of faith to be saved and raise their child in faith (1 Corinthians 7:14). Nevertheless, it is not true that a child cannot be unconditionally saved simply because parents of the child had no faith.

Here, you can experience the love of God again. Genesis 25 shows us that God foreknew Jacob would be greater in the future than his elder brother Esau when they fought together in their mother's womb. The omniscient God leads all the children who die before the age of five to salvation according to the judgment of conscience. This is possible because God knows whether the children would accept the Lord, if they were to live beyond those years, when they hear the gospel later on in their lives.

However, children whose parents have no faith and who do not pass the judgment of conscience as well inevitably fall into the Lower Grave belonging to Hell and would be tormented there.

The judgment of conscience and the faith of their parents

Children's salvation depends heavily on their parents' faith in this way. Thus, parents are to raise their children according to the will of God so that their children will not end up in Hell.

A long time ago, a certain couple that had had no child gave birth to a child with a vow in prayer. However, the child was killed prematurely in a traffic accident.

I could find the reason of their child's death in prayer. It was because the faith of the child's parents became cold and they were far away from God. The child could not attend the kindergarten affiliated with the church because his parents indulged in the worldly way of life. Accordingly, the child began to sing secular songs instead of songs praising God.

At that time, the child had the faith to receive salvation but he could not be saved if he were to grow under the influence of his parents. In this situation, God, through the traffic accident, called the child to eternal life and gave his parents an opportunity to repent. If the parents could have repented and returned to God without seeing their child violently killed, He would not have taken that measure.

Parents' responsibility for children's spiritual growth

Parents' faith has a direct influence on the salvation of their children. Children's faith cannot grow well if their parents have no concern for their children's spiritual growth leaving their children only to Sunday school.

Parents must pray for their children, examine if they always worship in spirit and true heart, and teach them to lead a life of prayer at home by being good examples to them.

I encourage all the parents to be awake in their own faith and raise their beloved children in the Lord. I bless that your family may enjoy the everlasting life together in Heaven.

Children from the Age of Six to Preteen Years

How can the children from the age of six to preteen years – about twelve years of age – be saved?

These children can understand the gospel when they hear it

33

and they can also decide what to believe by their own will and thought, not wholly but at least to a certain extent.

The age of children established here, of course, can be a bit different in each child's case because each child grows, develops, and matures at varying paces. The important factor is that normally by this age, children can believe in God by their own will and thought.

By their own faith regardless of their parents' faith

Children above six to twelve years of age have a good sense to choose faith. Therefore, they can be saved by their own faith regardless of the faith of their parents.

Your children, thus, can only go to Hell if you do not raise them in faith even if you yourself may have strong faith. There are children whose parents are non-believers. In such cases, it is more difficult for children to receive salvation.

The reason I distinguish the salvation of children prior to puberty years from after puberty years is because through God's abundant and overflowing love, the judgment of conscience may be applied to the former group.

God can give one more opportunity to these children to receive salvation because children of this age cannot decide on matters completely by their own will and thought since they are still under the influence of their parents.

Good children accept the Lord when they hear the gospel and receive the Holy Spirit. They also attend church but cannot attend church later on because of severe persecution from their parents who worship idols. However, by their early teen years, they can choose what is right and what is wrong by their own will regardless of parents' intention. They can maintain their faith if they truly believe in God no matter how severe the opposition and persecution of their parents may be.

Suppose a child, who could have had strong faith if he had been allowed to live longer, dies young. What, then, will happen to him? God will lead him to salvation by the law of the judgment of conscience because He knows the deepest of the child's heart.

However, if a child does not accept the Lord and does not pass the judgment of conscience, he or she will have no more opportunity and inevitably end up in Hell. Furthermore, it is understood that salvation of people beyond the puberty years is solely dependent on their own faith.

Children born in bad environments

Salvation of a mere child who can make no logical and sound judgment largely depends on spirits (nature, energy, or force) of parents and forefathers.

A child can be born with some mental disorder or be possessed by demons from very early ages of life due to the wickedness and idolatry of his or her forefathers. This is because descendents are under the influence of their parents and forefathers.

Concerning this, Deuteronomy 5:9-10 warns us as follows:

You shall not worship them or serve them; for I, the LORD your God, am a jealous God, visiting the iniquity of the fathers on the children, and on the third and the fourth generations of those who hate Me, but showing lovingkindness to thousands, to those who love Me and

35

keep My commandments.

1 Corinthians 7:14 also observes that *"For the unbelieving husband is sanctified through his wife, and the unbelieving wife is sanctified through her believing husband; for otherwise your children are unclean, but now they are holy."*

Likewise, it is very difficult for children to be saved if their parents do not live in faith.

Since God is love, He does not turn away from those who call His name even if they might have been born with wicked nature from their parents and forefathers. They can be led to salvation because God answers their prayers when they repent, try to live by His Word at all times, and call His name persistently.

Hebrews 11:6 tells us that *"And without faith it is impossible to please Him, for he who comes to God must believe that He is and that He is a rewarder of those who seek Him."* Even if people were born with evil nature, God changes their evil nature into good one and leads them to Heaven when they delight Him with good deeds and sacrifices in faith.

Those who cannot seek God on their own

Some people cannot seek God in faith because they have mental disorder or are possessed by demons. What, then, should they do?

In such a case, their parents or family members must demonstrate an adequate magnitude of faith on behalf of those people before God. The God of love will then open the door of salvation, seeing their faith and sincerity.

Parents are to blame for their child's destiny if the child dies before he has an opportunity to receive salvation. Thus, I urge you to understand that living in faith is very important for not only the parents themselves but also their offspring.

You should also understand the heart of God who values one soul more than the whole world. I encourage you to have an abundant love to look after not only your children but also children of your neighbors and relatives in faith.

Were Adam and Eve Saved?

Adam and Eve were driven out to the earth after they ate from the tree of the knowledge of good and evil in disobedience and they never heard the gospel. Were they saved? Let me explain whether the first man Adam and Eve received salvation.

Adam and Eve disobeyed God

In the beginning, God made the first man Adam and Eve in His own image and loved them very much. God prepared all things in advance for their abundant living and led them into the Garden of Eden. There, Adam and Eve lacked nothing.

Furthermore, God gave Adam great power and authority to govern all things in the universe. Adam governed all living things on earth, in the sky, and under the water. The enemy Satan and devil could not dare to enter the Garden because it was guarded and protected under the leadership of Adam.

Walking with them, God Himself provided them with spiritual education ever so kindly – the way a father would teach his beloved children everything from A to Z. Adam and

Eve lacked nothing but they were tempted by the cunning serpent and ate the forbidden fruit.

They came to taste the death in accordance with the Word of God that they would surely die (Genesis 2:17). In other words, their spirit died although they had been living spirits. As a result, they were driven out to the earth from the beautiful Garden of Eden. The human cultivation began on this cursed land and all things on it were cursed at the same time.

Were Adam and Eve saved? Some people may think that they could not receive salvation because all things were cursed and their descendents have been suffering due to their disobedience in the first place. Nevertheless, the God of love has left the door of salvation opened even for them.

Adam and Eve's thorough repentance

God forgives you so long as you repent wholeheartedly and return to Him even if you are tainted with all kinds of the original sin and actual sins committed while living in this world full of darkness and wickedness. God forgives you so long as you repent in your deep heart and return to Him even if you had been a murderer.

Comparing with today's people, you would know that Adam and Eve had truly pure and good hearts. Furthermore, God Himself taught them with tender love for a long period of time. Then, how would God send Adam and Eve to Hell without forgiving them once they repented from the depth of their hearts?

Adam and Eve suffered so much while they were being cultivated on the earth. They had been able to live in peace and always eat all kinds of fruit at any time in the Garden of Eden;

now, they could not eat without toil and sweat. Eve was to give birth with greater pain. They shed tears and suffered from grief resulting from their sins. Adam and Eve also witnessed one of their sons getting murdered by the other.

How much would they have missed their life under the protection and love of God in the Garden of Eden when they experienced such agony in this world? When they lived in the Garden, they did not recognize their happiness and did not thank God because they took their life, abundance, and God's love for granted.

However, now they could understand how happy they had been at that time and they came to thank God for the overflowing love He had given them. Eventually, they thoroughly repented of their sins of the past.

God opened the door of salvation for them

The wages of sin is death, but God who governs with love and justice forgives sin so long as people repent thoroughly.

The God of love allowed Adam and Eve to enter Heaven after receiving their repentance. However, they were barely saved to live in Paradise because God is also just. Their sin – forsaking God's great love – was not a trivial one. Adam and Eve have become responsible for necessitating the human cultivation as well as suffering, pain, and death of their descendants because of their disobedience.

Even if God's providence had allowed Adam and Eve to eat from the tree of the knowledge of good and evil, this very act of disobedience brought countless people to suffering and death. Therefore, Adam and Eve could not enter a better place within Heaven than Paradise and of course, they could not receive any glorious reward.

God works with love and justice

Let us think about God's love and justice through the case of the apostle Paul.

The apostle Paul used to be the main leader to persecute believers of Jesus and imprisoned them when he did not know Jesus correctly. When Stephen was martyred while he was witnessing the Lord, Paul watched as Stephen was stoned to death and considered it right.

However, Paul met the Lord and accepted Him on the way to Damascus. At that time, the Lord told him that he would be an apostle for the Gentiles and suffer greatly. Since then, the apostle Paul repented thoroughly and sacrificed the rest of his life for the Lord.

He could enter New Jerusalem because he carried out his mission with joy despite much suffering, and was faithful enough to give up his life for the Lord.

It is the law of nature to reap as you sow in this world. It is the same in the spiritual world. You will reap goodness if you have sown goodness and you will reap evil if you have sown evil.

As you can see through Paul's case, therefore, you must guard your heart, stay awake, and keep in mind that trials will follow you for your evil deeds from the past even if you are forgiven of them by repenting earnestly.

What Happened to the First Murderer Cain?

What happened to the first murderer Cain, who died

without ever hearing the gospel? Let us examine whether or not he was saved by the judgment of conscience.

Brothers Cain and Abel gave offering to God

Adam and Eve gave birth to children on the earth after they had been driven out of the Garden of Eden: Cain was their first son and Abel was Cain's younger brother. When they grew up, they gave offering to God. Cain brought some of the fruits of the soil as an offering to God but Abel brought fat portions from some of the firstborn of his flock.

God looked with favor on Abel and his offering but not on Cain and his offering. Then why did God look with favor on Abel and his offering?

You must not give offering to God against His will. According to the law of the spiritual world, you should worship God with the blood of sacrifice that can forgive sins. Therefore, in Old Testament times, people sacrificed oxen or lambs to worship God and in New Testament times, Jesus the Lamb of God became an atoning sacrifice by shedding His blood.

God accepts you with pleasure, answers your prayer, and blesses you when you worship Him with the sacrificing blood, that is, only when you worship Him in spirit. Spiritual sacrifice means worshipping God in spirit and in truth. God does not receive your worship with pleasure if you doze off or hear the message in idle thoughts during worship services.

God looked with favor only on Abel and his offering

Adam and Eve naturally knew very well spiritual law concerning the law of sacrificing offering because God had taught the law to them in the Garden of Eden for a long period of time while walking with them. Of course, they must have surely taught their children on how to give proper offering to God.

On the one hand, Abel worshipped God with the sacrificing blood in obedience to his parents' teaching. On the other hand, Cain did not bring the sacrificing offering but brought some of the fruits of the soil as an offering to God by his own reasoning.

Concerning this, Hebrews 11:4 says, *"By faith Abel offered to God a better sacrifice than Cain, through which he obtained the testimony that he was righteous, God testifying about his gifts, and through faith, though he is dead, he still speaks."*

God accepted Abel's offering because he spiritually worshipped God in obedience to His will with faith. However, God did not accept Cain's offering because he did not worship Him in spirit but he only worshipped Him according to his own standards and methods.

Cain killed Abel out of envy

Seeing that God accepted only his brother's offering but not his, Cain was very angry and his face was downcast. Finally, he attacked Abel and killed him.

Within only one generation since the human cultivation began on this earth, disobedience conceived envy, envy conceived greed and hatred, and greed and hatred blossomed into murder. How terrible is this?

You can see how rapidly people contaminate their hearts with sin once they allow sin in their hearts. This is why you should not allow even a trivial sin to enter your heart but remove it immediately.

What happened to the first murderer Cain? Some people

argue that Cain could not have been saved because he killed his righteous brother Abel.

Cain knew who God was through his parents. Compared with today's people, people in Cain's days inherited a relatively light original sin from their parents. Cain, even though he killed his brother in an instant out of envy, was also clean in his conscience.

Therefore, even if he had committed a murder, Cain could repent through God's punishment and God showed mercy on him.

Cain was saved after thorough repentance

In Genesis 4:13-15, Cain pleads with God that his punishment is too heavy and asks for His mercy when he was cursed and became a restless wanderer on the earth. God replied, *"Therefore whoever kills Cain, vengeance will be taken on him sevenfold"* and God placed a mark on Cain so that no one could kill him.

Here, you must realize how thoroughly Cain repented after killing his brother. Only then, could he have a way to communicate with God and would God put a mark on him as a token of His forgiveness. If Cain were a lost cause and destined to end up in Hell, then why would God hear Cain's plea in the first place, much less put a mark on him?

Cain had to be a restless wanderer on the earth as the punishment for killing his brother but in the end received salvation through the repentance of his sin. However, as in Adam's case, Cain was barely saved and allowed to live on the outer rim – not even the center – in Paradise.

The God of justice could not allow Cain to enter a better

place within Heaven beyond Paradise despite his repentance. Even if Cain lived in a comparatively much cleaner and less-sinful age, he was still wicked enough to kill his own brother.

Nonetheless, Cain might have been able to enter a better place in Heaven if he had been cultivated his evil heart to a good one and had done his best to please God with all his strength and all his heart. Yet, Cain's conscience was not even that good and pure.

Why does God not punish wicked people immediately?

You can have many questions while you are leading a life of faith. Some people are very wicked but God does not punish them. Others suffer from diseases or die because of their wickedness. Still others die at a young age even though they seem to be very faithful to God.

For example, King Saul was wicked enough in heart to try to kill David even though he knew that God had anointed David. Still, God left King Saul unpunished. As a result, Saul persecuted David even more.

This was an example of the providence of God's love. God wanted to train David to make him a big vessel and finally to make him king through the evil Saul. This is why King Saul died when God's discipline of David was completed.

Likewise, depending on each individual, God punishes people immediately or permits them to live unpunished. Everything contains the providence and love of God.

You should long for a better place in Heaven

In John 11:25-26, Jesus said, *"I am the resurrection and the life; he who believes in Me will live even if he dies, and everyone who lives and believes in Me will never die. Do you believe this?"*

Those who received salvation through accepting the gospel would surely resurrect, put on spiritual body, and enjoy the everlasting glory in Heaven. Those who are still alive on the earth will be caught up in the cloud to meet the Lord in the air when He descends from Heaven. The more you resemble the image of God, the better place in Heaven you will occupy.

On this, Jesus tells us in Matthew 11:12 that *"From the days of John the Baptist until now the kingdom of Heaven suffers violence, and violent men take it by force."* Jesus gave us another promise in Matthew 16:27, *"For the Son of Man is going to come in the glory of His Father with His angels, and will then repay every man according to his deeds."* 1 Corinthians 15:41 also observes that *"There is one glory of the sun, and another glory of the moon, and another glory of the stars; for star differs from star in glory."*

You cannot help longing for a better place within Heaven. You ought to try to become holier and more faithful in all God's house so that you will be allowed to enter New Jerusalem where the Throne of God is located. Like a farmer at harvest, God wants to lead as many people as possible to a better kingdom of Heaven through the human cultivation on the earth.

You have to know the spiritual world well to enter Heaven

People who did not know God and Jesus Christ could hardly enter New Jerusalem even though they were saved through the judgment of conscience.

There are people who do not clearly know the providence

45

of the human cultivation, the heart of God, and the spiritual world even though they have heard the gospel. Therefore, they neither know that the forceful men lay hold of the kingdom of Heaven nor do they have any hope for New Jerusalem.

God tells us to *"Be faithful until death, and I will give you the crown of life"* (Revelation 2:10). God abundantly rewards you in Heaven according to what you have sown. The reward is very precious because it lasts and remains glorious eternally.

When you keep this in your mind, you can prepare yourself well as a beautiful bride of the Lord like the five wise virgins and accomplish the whole spirit.

1 Thessalonians 5:23 reads, *"Now may the God of peace Himself sanctify you completely; and may your spirit whole soul, and body be preserved blameless, at the coming of our Lord Jesus Christ."*

Therefore, you must diligently prepare yourself as a bride of the Lord to accomplish the whole spirit before the return of the Lord Jesus Christ, or God's calling of your soul whichever may come first.

It is not enough to come to church every Sunday and confess, "I believe." You must get rid of any kind of evil and be faithful in all houses of God. The more you please God, the better place in Heaven you will be able to enter.

I encourage you to become a true child of God with this knowledge. In the name of the Lord, I pray you to not only walk with the Lord here on the earth but also live closer to the Throne of God in Heaven forever and ever.

Chapter 3

The Lower Grave and the Identity of the Messengers of Hell

At harvest every year, farmers are joyful with the expectation of good crops. However, it is difficult for them to harvest first-rate wheat all the time even though they work arduously day after day, night after night, planting fertilizers, weeding out, and so forth. Among the crop, there would be second-rate, third-rate, and even the chaff.

People cannot eat the chaff as their food. Besides, the chaff cannot be gathered together with the wheat because the chaff will spoil the wheat. This is why the farmer gathers the chaff and burns it up or uses it as manure.

It is the same with God's human cultivation on the earth. God seeks true children who also have the holy and perfect image of God. However, there are some people who do not get rid of their sins thoroughly or others who are entirely consumed by evil and lose the duty of man. God wants holy and true children but He also gathers into Heaven even those who died before completely getting rid of their sins so long as they tried to live in faith.

On the one hand, God does not send people to the terrifying Hell if they have the faith of the size of a mustard seed to depend on the blood of Jesus Christ regardless of His original purpose to cultivate and collect only the true children. On the other hand, those who do not believe in Jesus Christ and fight against God to the end have no other option but to go to Hell because they have chosen the way of destruction by their evil within themselves.

Then, how would unsaved souls be led into the Lower Grave and how would they be punished there? I will explain in detail the Lower Grave belonging to Hell and the identity of messengers of hell.

The Messengers of Hell Take People to the Lower Grave

On the one hand, when a saved person with faith dies, two angels come to lead him to the Upper Grave belonging to Heaven. In Luke 24:4, we find two angels waiting for Jesus after His burial and resurrection. On the other hand, when an unsaved person dies, two messengers of hell come to lead him to the Lower Grave. It is usually possible to know whether a person on his or her deathbed is saved or not by observing the person's facial expression.

Before the moment of death

People's spiritual eyes are opened before the moment of death. The person dies peacefully with a smile if he or she sees angels in light and the dead corpse does not stiff soon. Even after two or three days, the dead body does not rot or give out bad odor, and the person appears to be still alive.

How, however, terrible and trembling must unsaved people

feel to see the horrific messengers of hell? They die in terrible fear, unable to close their eyes.

If one's salvation is not certain, angels and messengers of hell fight each other to take that soul to their respective place. That is why the person is so anxious until death. How fearful and anxious would he be when he sees messengers of hell bring charges against him, constantly saying, "He has no faith to be saved"?

When a man of weak faith is on his deathbed, people with strong faith should help him have more faith through worship and praise. He then may receive salvation even on his deathbed by having faith, even though he only receives the shameful salvation and ends up in Paradise.

You can see the man on his deathbed becoming peaceful because he receives faith to be saved while people worship and praise for him. When a man of strong faith is on his deathbed, you do not need to help him to grow or have faith. It is better to give him hope and joy.

A Waiting Place to the World of Evil Spirits

On the one hand, even a person with very weak faith can be saved if he has faith through worship and praise on his deathbed. On the other hand, if he is not saved, messengers of hell lead him to the waiting place belonging to the Lower Grave and he is to adjust himself to the world of evil spirits.

Just as saved souls have three days of an adjusting period in the Upper Grave, unsaved souls also stay for three days in the waiting place that resembles a great pit in the Lower Grave.

Three days of adjusting at the waiting place

The waiting place in the Upper Grave, where saved souls stay for three days, is full of jubilation, peace, and hope for the glorious life ahead. The waiting place in the Lower Grave, however, is just the opposite.

Unsaved souls would be living in unbearable pain, receiving various kinds of punishment according to their deeds in this world. Before falling into the Lower Grave, they prepare themselves for life in the world of evil spirits at the waiting place for three days. These three days in the waiting place is not peaceful but only the beginning of their perpetual painful life.

Various kinds of birds with big and pointed bills peck at these souls. These birds are very ugly and disgusting spiritual objects unlike the birds of this world.

Unsaved souls are already separated from their bodies and thus, you may think that they cannot feel any pain. Yet, these birds can hurt them because birds in the waiting place are also spiritual beings.

Whenever birds peck at the souls, their bodies are torn apart with bleeding and are skinned off as well. The souls try to dodge the pecking of birds but they cannot. They only struggle and crouch with shouts. Sometimes, birds come to pluck out their eyes.

Different Punishments in the Lower Grave for Different Sins

After the three days' stay in the waiting place, unsaved souls are allocated to different places of punishment in the

Lower Grave according to their sins from this world. Heaven is very spacious. Hell is also so spacious that there are countless separated places to accommodate unsaved souls even in the Lower Grave, which is only a part of Hell.

Different places of punishment

Overall, the Lower Grave is dark and humid, and souls can feel the sizzling heat there. Unsaved souls will be constantly tortured with beating, pecking, and tearing.

In this world, when your leg or arm is cut off, you have to live without your leg or arm. Once you die, your agony and trouble would be gone with your death. In the Lower Grave, however, if you have your neck cut off, your neck will regenerate itself. Even if you have a part of your body cut off, your body will soon be made a whole. Just as you cannot slice water with the sharpest sword or knife, no torture, pecking, or ripping body parts into pieces can end the agony.

Your eyes will be restored soon after birds peck at them. Even if you are wounded and your intestines gushed out, you would soon be restored. Your blood will be shed without an end while you are tormented, but you cannot die there because blood would be soon filled up again. This horrific pattern torments you repeatedly.

That is why there is a river of blood originating from the shedding of blood of souls in the Lower Grave. Remember that a spirit is immortal. When it is repeatedly tortured forever and ever, its pain lasts forever as well. Souls beg for death but they cannot and are not allowed to die. From ceaseless tortures, the Lower Grave is full of people's screaming, groans, and bloody rotting smell.

Agonizing cries in the Lower Grave

I assume that some of you have directly experienced war. If not, you may have seen horrific scenes depicting cries and pain in war movies or historical documentaries. Wounded people are here and there. Some of them lose their legs or arms. Their eyes are shattered and even the contents of their brains are blasted out. Nobody knows when artillery fire would rain on him or her. That place is full of the suffocating smoke of the artillery, bloody odor, groans, and screams. People may call such a sight a "Hell on earth."

However, this disastrous scene of the Lower Grave is far more miserable than the worst scene on any battlefield in this world. Furthermore, souls in the Lower Grave suffer not only from present torture but also from the fear of tortures to come.

The torment is too much for them and they try to escape it in vain. Furthermore, what await them are only the blazing fire and the sulfur of the deeper Hell.

How regrettable and deploring souls would be when they watch the burning sulfur of Hell, saying, "I should have believed when they proclaimed the gospel... I should not have sinned...!" However, there is no second chance and there is no way of salvation for them.

Lucifer in Charge of the Lower Grave

One cannot possibly fathom the kind and magnitude of punishment in the Lower Grave. Just as methods of torture vary in this world, the same can be said of tortures in the Lower Grave.

Some may suffer from having their bodies getting rotten. Others may get their bodies eaten or chewed on and blood sucked by various bugs and insects. Still others are pressed against blazingly hot stones or remain standing on sands with the temperature seven times higher than those found on beaches or deserts in this world. In some cases, the messengers of hell themselves torture souls. Other torture methods involve water, fire, and other unimaginable methods and equipment.

The God of love does not rule this place for unsaved souls. God has given the evil spirits the authority to reign over this place. The head of all evil spirits, Lucifer, rules the Lower Grave, where unsaved souls like the chaff are to stay. There is no mercy or pity here, and Lucifer has control over every aspect of the Lower Grave.

The identity of Lucifer, head of all evil spirits

Who is Lucifer? Lucifer had been one of the archangels, whom God loved very much and called her the "son of the dawn" (Isaiah 14:12). Nonetheless, she rebelled against God and became the head of evil spirits.

Angels in Heaven do not have humanity and free will. Therefore, they cannot choose things by their will and they only follow commands like robots. However, God especially gives some angels humanity and shares love with them. Lucifer, who was one of such angels, was responsible for the heavenly music. Lucifer praised God with her beautiful voice and musical instruments and pleased God with singing the glory of God.

However, she gradually became arrogant because of God's special love for her and her desire to become higher and more powerful than God led her to rebel against Him in the end.

Lucifer challenged and rebelled against God

The Bible tells us that a tremendous amount of angels followed Lucifer (2 Peter 2:4; Jude 1:6). There is a myriad of angels in Heaven and about one third of them followed Lucifer. You can imagine how many angels joined Lucifer. Lucifer rebelled against God in her arrogance.

How was it possible for countless angels to follow Lucifer? You can understand this easily if you think about the fact that angels only obey commands the way machines or robots do.

First, Lucifer won the support of some head angels, who were under her influence, and then she easily won subordinate angels under those head angels.

Besides the angels, dragons and a part of cherubim among spiritual beings also followed Lucifer's rebellion. Lucifer, who challenged God in rebellion, after all, was defeated and cast off with her followers from Heaven where she originally was. Then they were imprisoned in the Abyss until they were to be used for the human cultivation.

How you have fallen from heaven, O star of the morning, son of the dawn! You have been cut down to the earth, You who have weakened the nations! But you said in your heart, "I will ascend to heaven; I will raise my throne above the stars of God, and I will sit on the mount of assembly In the recesses of the north. I will ascend above the heights of the clouds; I will make myself like the Most High." Nevertheless you will be thrust down to Sheol, to the recesses of the pit (Isaiah 14:12-15).

Lucifer was beautiful beyond description while she was in Heaven with God's overflowing love. After the rebellion, however, she turned ugly and horrific.

People who saw her with their spiritual eyes say that Lucifer is so ugly that you will find her revolting even if you only saw her. She looks dreary with her disheveled hair dyed in various colors such as red, white, and yellow, soaring high into the sky.

Today, Lucifer leads people to imitate her in dress and hairstyle. When people dance, they are very wild, tumultuous, and ugly, pointing their fingers.

These are the trends of our times Lucifer creates and they proliferate through mass media and culture. These trends can hurt people's emotion and lead them to chaos. Furthermore, these trends delude people to distance themselves from God and even deny Him.

Children of God should be different and not fall into worldly trends. If you fell into worldly trends, you would naturally keep the love of God away from you because worldly trends take away your heart and thought (1 John 2:15).

Evil spirits make the Lower Grave a dreadful place

On the one hand, the God of love is goodness itself. He is preparing all things for us in His wise and good thought and judgment. He wants us to live perpetually in utmost happiness in the beautiful Heaven. On the other hand, Lucifer is evil itself. Evil spirits as followers of Lucifer are always thinking of ways to torment people more severely. In their evil wisdom, they make the Lower Grave even a more terrifying place by devising all kinds of torturing methods.

Even in this world, throughout history people devise various cruel methods of torture. When Korea was under the rule of Japan, the Japanese tortured Korean leaders of national independence movements by piercing beneath their fingernails with a bamboo needle or pulling off their fingernails or toenails one by one. They also poured a mixture of red pepper and water into the eyes and nostrils of the movement leaders while they were hanged upside down. Revolting smell of burning flesh overwhelmed the torturing room because Japanese torturers scorched various parts of their bodies with hot pieces of metal. Their internal organs gushed out of their stomachs as they were beaten severely.

How did people torment criminals throughout Korean history? They would twist a criminal's legs as a form of torture. The criminal was bound about the ankles and the knees and then two sticks were inserted between his two calves. The bones in the legs of the criminal were shattered into pieces as the tormenter moved the two sticks. Can you imagine how painful that must have been?

The tortures carried out by men are as cruel as our own imagination takes us. Then, how much more cruel and miserable would it be when the evil spirits with far more powerful wisdom and ability torture unsaved souls? It is their pleasure to develop various methods of torture and put unsaved souls subject to them.

This is why you must know the world of evil spirits. Then you can rule, control, and overcome them. You can easily defeat them when you keep yourself holy and clean without conforming to the patterns of this world.

The Identity of Messengers of Hell

Who are these messengers of hell torturing unsaved people in the Lower Grave? They are fallen subordinate angels who followed Lucifer in rebellion before the world began.

And angels who did not keep their own domain, but abandoned their proper abode, He has kept in eternal bonds under darkness for the judgment of the great day (Jude 1:6).

The fallen angels cannot come out to the world freely because God has bound them in the darkness until the Judgment of the Great White Throne. Some people assert that demons are the fallen angels but that is not true. Demons are unsaved souls who are released from the Lower Grave to do their work under special circumstances. I will explain this in detail in chapter 8.

Angels who had fallen with Lucifer

God bound the fallen angels in the darkness – Hell – for the Judgment. Thus, the fallen angels cannot come out to the world except only on special occasions.

They had been very beautiful until they rebelled against God. However, the messengers of hell have been neither beautiful nor brilliant ever since they fell and were cursed.

They look so dreary that you will be disgusted with them. Their image is similar to faces of human beings, or they look like of various detestable animals.

Their appearances are similar to those of detestable animals such as pigs written in the Bible (Leviticus 11). But they have cursed, ugly images. They also decorate their bodies with grotesque colors and patterns.

They wear iron armor and military shoes. Sharp instruments of torture are fixed firmly on their bodies. They often have a knife, a spear, or a whip in their hands.

They assume a domineering attitude and you can feel their strong power when they move about because they are exercising their complete power and authority in the darkness. People are very fearful of demons. But, the messengers of hell are more horrifying than demons.

Messengers of Hell torture souls

What exactly is the role of the messengers of hell? It is primarily to torture unsaved souls as they take charge of Hell.

More explicit tortures performed by the messengers of hell are reserved for those with heavier punishments in the Lower Grave. For example, an ugly pig-shaped messenger of hell slices the souls' bodies or inflates them like balloons and pops or whips them.

In addition, they torture people with various methods. Even children cannot be excluded from torture. What makes our spirits broken is the fact that the messengers of hell prick or beat children for amusement. Therefore, you should do your best to prevent even a soul from falling into Hell which is a cruel, miserable, and horrible place filled with never-ending pain and suffering.

I was at the threshold of death from excessive stress and overworking in 1992. At that moment, God showed me many of my church members following the patterns of this world. I hoped eagerly to be with the Lord until I saw this scene. But I could no longer want to be with the Lord because I knew that many of my sheep would fall into Hell.

Thus, I changed my mind and asked God to revive me. God gave me strength in an instant and to my surprise, I was able to get up from my deathbed and became perfectly healthy. The power of God revived me. Because I know so well and so much about Hell, I diligently proclaim the secrets of Hell God has revealed to me in hopes of saving even one more soul.

Chapter 4

Punishments in the Lower Grave on Unsaved Children

In the previous chapter, I described how the fallen archangel Lucifer governs Hell and how other fallen angels rule under Lucifer's leadership. The messengers of hell torture unsaved souls according to their sins. Generally, the punishment in the Lower Grave is divided into four levels. The lightest punishment is inflicted upon people who fall into Hell as a result of the judgment of conscience. The heaviest punishment is inflicted upon people whose consciences are branded as with hot iron and who confronted God the way Judas Iscariot did by selling Jesus for his personal gain.

In subsequent chapters, I will explain in detail the kinds of punishments inflicted upon unsaved souls in the Lower Grave belonging to Hell. Before delving into punishments inflicted upon adults, I will discuss the kinds of punishments inflicted upon unsaved children by different age groups.

Fetus and Suckling

Even a thoughtless child can go to the Lower Grave if he could not pass the judgment of conscience because of the sinful nature within him inherited from his unbelieving parents. The child would receive a relatively light punishment because his sin is light when compared to that of an adult but he still suffers from hunger and unbearable pain.

Sucklings cry and suffer from hunger

Weaning babies who cannot yet walk or talk are separately categorized and confined in a large place. They cannot think, move, or walk on their own because unsaved babies maintain the same feature and conscience they possess at the moment of their death.

Furthermore, they do not know why they are in Hell because they do not have any knowledge registered in their brains. They just cry from hunger by nature without knowing their mothers and fathers. A messenger of hell would prick an infant's belly, arm, leg, eye, fingernail, or toenail with a pointed object that resembles a gimlet. The baby then lets out a shrill cry and the messenger of hell just laughs at the baby with pleasure. Even though they cry constantly, no one takes care of these babies. Their crying continues through exhaustion and severe pain. Furthermore, the messengers of hell sometimes gather around, pick up one baby, and blow air into the baby like a balloon. They then throw, kick, or play catch with the baby for fun. How cruel and horrible is this?

Deserted fetuses are robbed of warmth and comfort

What is the fate of fetuses who die before they are born? As I already explained, most of them are saved but there are some exceptions. Some fetuses cannot be saved because they are conceived with the worst nature inherited from their parents who had seriously turned against God and did extremely evil deeds. The souls of unsaved fetuses are also confined in one place like the one with weaning infants.

They are not tortured as severely as souls of older people because they had no conscience and committed no sin by the moment of their death. Their punishment and curse are that they are left abandoned without the warmth or the comfort they felt in their mothers' wombs.

Body frames in the Lower Grave

In what shapes are unsaved souls in the Lower Grave? On the one hand, if a weaning child dies, he is confined there in the shape of a weaning child. If a fetus dies in his mother's womb, he is confined in the Lower Grave in the shape of a fetus. On the other hand, saved souls in Heaven will put on newly resurrected body at the second coming of Jesus Christ although they have the same shape as in this world. At that time, everybody will be transformed into a beautiful thirty-three-year-old person like the Lord Jesus and will put on spiritual body. A short person will have the most optimal height and a person missing a leg or an arm will have his or her body parts restored.

However, unsaved souls in Hell cannot put on new, resurrected body even after the Second Advent of the Lord. They cannot resurrect because they have no life obtained from Jesus Christ and thus, they are in the same shape they had at the time of their death. Their faces and bodies are pale and dark-blue – like corpses – and their hair disheveled because of horror in Hell. Some wear rags, others only a few pieces of cloth, and still others have nothing to cover their bodies.

In Heaven, saved souls wear beautiful white robes and bright crowns. In addition, the brightness of robes and decorations are different in accordance with each one's glory and prize. Conversely, in Hell, appearances of unsaved souls are different according to the magnitude and kinds of their sins.

Toddlers

Newborn babies grow and learn to stand up, toddle, and utter a few words. When these toddlers die, what kinds of punishments will be inflicted upon them?

Toddlers are also grouped in one place. They are suffering instinctively because they were not able to think logically or judge things sensibly at the time of their death.

Toddlers cry for their parents in unbearable horror

Toddlers are only two to three years old. Thus, they do not recognize even their death and do not know why they are in Hell, but they still remember their mothers and fathers. That is why they cry repeatedly, "Where are you, mommy? Daddy? I want to go home! Why am I here?"

While they were living in this world, their mothers came quickly and held them tightly in their bosom when, for instance, they fell and scraped their knees. However, their mothers do not come to comfort them even if they shout and cry when their bodies are drenched in blood. Does not a child shout in tears with fear when he loses his mother at a supermarket or at a department store?

They cannot find their parents who will protect them from this horrible Hell. This fact alone is fearful enough to lead them to unbearable horror. Furthermore, threatening voices and grotesque laughter of messengers of hell force babies to shout in tears even louder but all is useless.

To kill time, the messengers of hell slap the back of toddlers, and trample or whip them. Then toddlers, in shock and pain, try to crouch or run away from them. However, in such a crowded place, the toddlers cannot run away and in a muddle of tears and snivel, they are entangled with one another, trampled on, and bruised and torn to shed blood all over the place. Under these miserable circumstances, children constantly cry in tears because they long for their mothers, are hungry and horrified. Such conditions alone are "Hell" for these babies.

It is hardly possible for children of two or three years of age to have committed serious sins and crimes. Despite this fact, they are miserably punished like this due to their original sin and self-committed sins. Then how much more miserably would adults, who commit more serious sins than children, be punished in Hell?

However, anyone can be free from the punishment of Hell only if he accepts Jesus Christ who died on the cross and redeemed us, and lives in the light. He can be led into Heaven since he is forgiven of sins of the past, the present, and the future.

Children Old Enough to Walk and Talk

Toddlers, who begin to walk and utter one or two words, run and speak well when they reach the age of three years.

What kinds of punishments would these toddlers, from three to five years of age, receive in the Lower Grave?

Messengers of Hell chase them with spears

Children from the age of three to five are separated in a dark and spacious place and left to be punished there. They run away with all their might to everywhere they can in order to avoid messengers of hell chasing them with three-pronged spears in their hands.

A three-pronged spear is a spear whose end is divided into three parts. The messengers of hell are chasing the souls of these children, piercing them with the spears the way a hunter runs after his game. At last, these children reach a cliff, and far down the cliff, they see water boiling like lava from an active volcano. At first, these children hesitate to jump down from the cliff but are forced to jump into the boiling water to avoid the messengers of hell chasing them. They have no other option.

Struggling to get out of the boiling water

Children can avoid the piercing of spears in the hands of the messengers, but now they are in the boiling water. Can you possibly imagine how painful this must be? Children struggle to get even their faces above the boiling water, since it enters their nostrils and mouths. When the messengers see this, they tease the children, saying, "Isn't this fun?" or "Oh, this is so delightful!" Then the messengers shout, "Who let these children fall into Hell? Let's lead their parents to the way of death, bring them here when they die, and make them watch their children suffering and being tormented!"

Just then, the children struggling to escape the boiling water are caught in a large net as fish caught in a net and flung back to the original place from which they began running away. From this time on, the painful process of the children's running away from messengers of hell chasing with spears and their jumping down into the boiling water is repeated time and again without an end.

These children are only three to five years of age; they cannot run very well. Yet, they try to run as fast as they can to avoid the chasing of messengers of hell who trail them with spears and they get to the cliff. They jump down into the boiling water and again struggle to get out of it. They are then caught in a large net and flung back to the original place. This routine is repeated endlessly. How miserable and tragic this is!

Have you ever burned your finger from a hot iron or a hotpot? You may then know how hot and painful that was. Now, imagine that your whole body is drenched with boiling water, or that you are submerged in the boiling water in a large pot. It is painful and terrible even to think about it.

If you have ever had a third-degree burn, you may remember well how extremely painful that was. You may also remember the ruddy inner flesh, the burning odor of the flesh, and the terrible and foul smell of the rotting of dead cells in that burnt flesh.

Even if the burnt part is healed, ugly scars often remain. Most people have difficulty in having fellowships with people with such scars. Sometimes, even the victim's family members find themselves unable to dine with him. During times of treatment, the patient may not endure the scraping of the burned flesh, and in the worst of cases, such a patient develops mental disorders or commits suicide because of the stifling sensation and the agony involved in the treatment. If a child suffers from a burn, his parents' hearts also feel the pain.

Yet, the worst of burn in this world is not comparable to the punishments the souls of unsaved toddlers will receive in Hell repeatedly with no end. The magnitude of pain and cruelty these punishments thrust upon these children in Hell is simply beyond our imagination.

Nowhere to run or hide from these recurring punishments

Children run and run to avoid the messengers of hell who chase them with three-pronged spears in their hands, and they fall into the boiling water from a dead-end cliff. They are completely immersed in the boiling water. The boiling water sticks to the body like viscous lava and smells foul. Furthermore, the revolting and sticky boiling water enters their nostrils and mouths while they are struggling to get out of the pool of the boiling water. How is this comparable to any kind of burn in this world, no matter how serious it may be?

These children are not dull to senses even though they are repeatedly tormented without a break. They cannot go mad, faint to forget or become oblivious to the pain even for a little while, or commit suicide to avoid the pain in Hell. How miserable this is!

This is how children of about three, four, or five years of age suffer from such a tremendous amount of pain in the Lower Grave as a punishment for their sins. Can you, then, possibly imagine the kind and magnitude of punishments in store for older people in other parts of Hell?

Children from the Age of Six to Twelve

What kinds of punishments will be inflicted upon unsaved children from the age of six to twelve in the Lower Grave?

Buried by a river of blood

Since the creation of the world, countless unsaved souls have been shedding their blood while being terribly tormented in the Lower Grave. How much blood would they have shed especially since their arms and legs are restored as soon as they had been cut off?

The amount of their blood is sufficient to create a river because their punishment is repeated without an end regardless of the amount of blood already spilt. Even in this world, after a major war or massacre, people's blood forms a small pool or a little stream. In such a case, the air is filled with foul odor coming from the rotting blood. On hot summer days, the smell is worse, and all kinds of harmful insects swarm and infectious diseases become epidemic.

In the Lower Grave of Hell, there is not a small pool or a little stream but a wide and deep river of blood. Children of ages from about six to twelve are punished on the riverbank and buried there. The more serious the sin they have committed, the closer to the river and deeper they are buried.

Digging the ground

Children who are far away from the river of blood are not buried in the ground. Still, they are so hungry that they keep on digging the hard ground with their bare hands in search of something to eat. They desperately dig in vain until they lose their nails and their fingertips become all stubby. Their fingers are worn out to half of their original size and drenched in blood. Even the bones in their fingers are exposed. Eventually, their palms as well as their fingers become worn out. Yet, despite this pain, these children are forced to dig in a faint hope of finding food.

As you approach closer to the river, you can easily detect that children are more evil. The more evil the children are, the closer to the river they are placed. They even fight one another to bite off the other's flesh in extreme hunger while buried to their waistline in the ground.

The most evil children are punished right by the shores of the river and they are buried up to their neck in the ground. People in this world will eventually die if they are buried up to their neck in the ground, because the blood cannot circulate throughout the body. The fact that there is no death only means an endless agony for the unsaved souls punished in Hell.

They suffer from the foul odor of the river. All kinds of harmful insects like mosquitoes or flies from the river bite the children's faces but they cannot swat the insects because they are buried in the ground. Finally, their faces become swollen to the extent that they are no longer recognizable.

Miserable children: toys of messengers of hell

This is not by any means the end of the children's suffering. Their eardrums may be ruptured because of loud laughter of the messengers of hell as they rest at the riverbank, laughing and talking with one another. The messengers of hell, when they rest, also trample or sit on the heads of these children buried in the ground.

Clothes and shoes of the messengers of hell are equipped with sharpest objects. Thus, children's heads are crushed, their faces shredded, or their hairs are pulled away in lumps when the messengers trample or sit on these children. Furthermore, the messengers slash children's faces or tread down their heads under their feet. How cruel a punishment is this?

You may wonder, "Is it possible for grade-school-aged children to have committed sins enough to receive such a cruel punishment?" However young these children may be, they have the original sin and sins they deliberately committed. The spiritual law, which dictates that "the wages of sin is death," is universally applicable to every person regardless of his or her age.

Youths Who Jeered at Prophet Elisha

2 Kings 2:23-24 portrays a scene in which Prophet Elisha from Jericho went up to Bethel. As the prophet walked along the road, some youths came from the city and jeered at him, saying "Go on up, you baldhead!" No longer able to endure them, Elisha at last cursed the children. Two female bears came out and "tore up forty-two" of these children. What do you suppose happened to the forty-two children in the Lower Grave?

Buried up to their neck

Two female bears tore up forty-two children. Then you can imagine how many children must have followed and jeered

71

at the prophet. Elisha was a prophet who performed many powerful works of God. In other words, Elisha could not have cursed them if they had mocked him only with a few words.

They kept on following and mocking him, saying, "Go on up, you baldhead!" Besides, they threw stones at him and pricked him with a stick. The prophet Elisha must have earnestly admonished and scolded them first, but he would have cursed them only because they were too wicked to be forgiven.

This incident took place several thousands years ago when people had much better conscience and evil did not prevail as much as it does in our times. Those children must have been wicked enough to mock and jeer at an old prophet like Elisha, who performed the powerful works of God.

In the Lower Grave, these children are punished near the river of blood while buried up to their neck. They suffocate from the foulest odor from the river, and are bitten by all kinds of harmful insects as well. In addition, they are cruelly tormented by the messengers of hell.

Parents must steer their children

How do children of our times behave? Some of them leave their friends out in the cold, take their allowance or lunch money, beat them, even burn them with cigarette butts – all because they do not like them. Some children even commit suicide because they can no longer endure such repeated and cruel harassments. Other children form organized gangs when they are only in elementary schools, and even kill people, imitating a notorious criminal.

Therefore, parents should raise their children in a way to

prevent them from conforming to the patterns of this world and instead lead them to develop and live a faithful life, fearing God. How terribly sorry will you be if you enter Heaven and see your children tormented in Hell? It is so ghastly even to think about it.

Thus, you ought to raise your precious children to live in faith in accordance with the truth. For example, you should teach your children not to talk or run around during a worship service, but pray and praise with all their heart, mind, and soul. Even infants, who cannot understand what their mothers say, sleep well without crying during worship services when their mothers pray for them and raise them in faith. These babies, too, will have a reward for their behavior in Heaven.

Children of the age from three or four can worship God and pray when parents teach them to make it a rule. Depending on the age, the depth of prayer may be different. Parents can teach their children to increase their time of prayer little by little, i.e. from five minutes to ten minutes, to thirty minutes, to an hour, and so forth.

However young these children may be, when parents teach them the word according to their age and the level of comprehension, and enlighten them to live according to it, the children will often try harder to adhere to the Word of God and live in a manner pleasing to Him. They will also repent and confess their sins in tears when the Holy Spirit works within them. I urge you to teach them concretely who Jesus Christ is and lead them to grow in faith.

Chapter 5

Punishments for People Who Die after Puberty Years

Anyone who enters Heaven will receive different rewards and glory according to his deeds in this life. Conversely, different punishments in the Lower Grave are inflicted upon an individual according to his evil deeds in this life. P eople in Hell suffer from a tremendous amount of lasting pain, and the severity of the pain and agony differs from that of one another depending on their own deeds in this life. A man, whether he ends up in Heaven or Hell, will reap what he sows.

The more sins you have committed, the deeper part of Hell you will enter, and the heavier your sins, the more agonizing your pain will be in Hell. Depending on how much one is contrary to the heart of God – in other words, how much one resembles the sinful nature of Lucifer – severity of punishments will be determined accordingly.

Galatians 6:7-8 tells us, *"Do not be deceived, God is not mocked; for whatever a man sows, this he will also reap. For the one who sows to his own flesh will from the flesh reap corruption, but the one who sows to the Spirit will from the Spirit reap eternal life."* In this manner, you will surely reap what you sow.

What kinds of punishments will people who die after puberty years receive in the Lower Grave? In this chapter, I will discuss four levels of punishments in the Lower Grave inflicted upon souls according to their deeds in this life. On a side note, please understand that I cannot provide graphic details because an extra weight will be added to the amount of your fear.

The First Level of Punishment

Some souls are forced to stand on sands that are seven times hotter than sands in the deserts or beaches of this world. They cannot escape from the suffering because it is as if they are stranded in the middle of a great desert.

Have you ever walked on burning hot sands, in bare feet, on a hot summer's day? You cannot even bear the pain even if you try to walk on a beach in bare feet on a hot, sunny, summer day for ten or fifteen minutes. Sands in tropical parts of the world are much hotter. Keep in mind that sands in the Lower Grave are seven times hotter than the hottest sands of this world.

During my pilgrimage to the Holy Land, instead of boarding a trolley, I tried running on the asphalt-paved road on the way to the Dead Sea. I began to run fast with two other pilgrims who accompanied me on the trip. At first, there was no pain but about the halfway through, I could feel burning sensations across both of my soles. Although we wanted to escape from the sufferings, there was no place to go; on either side of the road were fields of gravels, which were just as hot.

We ended up running to the other end of the road, at which point we were able to dip and soak our feet in the cold water of a swimming pool nearby. Fortunately, none of us had been burned. This running lasted only about ten minutes, and it was enough to bring an intolerable amount of pain. Imagine, then, that you will be *forced to* stand *eternally* on sands that are seven times hotter than any sands found on the earth. No matter how unbearably hot the sands are, there is certainly no possibility of reduction or end of the punishment. Yet, this is the lightest of all punishments in the Lower Grave.

There is another soul being tortured in a different way. He is forced to lie on a heavy rock, which has been heated red-hot, and receives the punishment of being roasted continuously without an end. The scene resembles meat being cooked on a sizzling grill. Just then, another rock that has also been heated red-hot is dropped on his body, crushing it and everything therein. Imagine any kind of clothing you iron: the ironing board is the rock on which the clothing – the condemned soul – is laid, and the iron is the second rock pressing down the clothing.

The heat is one part of the torture; body parts being crushed is quite another. Limbs are smashed into pieces by the pressure between the rocks. Its force is strong enough to shatter his ribs and internal organs. When his skull is crushed, eyeballs pop out and all the fluids from the skull gush out.

How can his suffering be described? Although he is a soul without a physical form, he can still feel and suffer the tremendous amount of pain the way he felt in this life. He is in lasting agony. Along with shrills of other souls being tormented, this soul, trapped in his own fear and horror, laments and cries out, "How can I escape from this torment?"

The Second Level of Punishment

Through the story of the rich man and Lazarus in Luke

16:19-31, we can get a glimpse of the wretchedness of the
Lower Grave. By the power of the Holy Spirit, I have heard a
lamentation of a man being tormented in the Lower Grave. By
listening to the following confession, I pray that you will wake
up from your spiritual slumber.

> I am dragged around here and there
> but there is no end.
> I run and run but there is no end.
> Nowhere can I find a place to hide.
> My skin is peeled off in this place,
> filled with the foulest odor.
> Insects are nibbling away my flesh.
> I try to run and run away from them,
> yet I am always at the same place.
> They are still biting and eating away my body;
> they are sucking my blood.
> I am trembling in terror and fear.
> What am I to do?

> Please, I beg you,
> let people know what is happening to me.
> Tell them of my torment
> so that they will not end up here.
> I really don't know what to do.
> Under the great fear and terror,
> I can only groan.
> It is useless to look for a refuge.
> They are scratching my back.
> They are biting on my arms.
> They are peeling off my skin.

They are eating my muscles away.
They are sucking my blood.
When this is over,
I will be thrust into to the lake of fire.
What can I do?
What am I to do?

Although I did not believe in Jesus as my Savior,
I thought I was a man of good conscience.
Until I was thrown into the Lower Grave,
I never realized I had committed so many sins!
Now, I can only regret and regret
for things I have done.
Please, make sure
there will not be any more people like me.
Many people here, while living,
thought they were leading good lives.
Yet, they are all here.
Many who professed to believe
and thought they were living
according to the will of God are also here,
and they are tortured more cruelly than I.

I wish I could faint to forget the sufferings
even for a while, but I cannot.
I cannot rest even though I close my eyes.
When I open my eyes,
nothing can be seen and nothing can be tangible.
While I keep on running away here and there,
I am still at the same place.
What can I do?

What am I to do?
I beg you, please make sure
that there will not be anyone else
following my footsteps!

This soul is a relatively good man, compared to many others in the Lower Grave. He is begging God to let people know what is happening to him. Even in this extreme torment, he is worried about souls who may end up there. The way the rich man begged for his brothers to be warned so that they would not "also come to this place of torment," this soul also is pleading with God (Luke 16).

However, those who fall into the third and fourth level of punishments in the Lower Grave do not have even this kind of goodness. So, they challenge God and blame others ruthlessly.

The Punishment on Pharaoh

Pharaoh, the king of Egypt who opposed Moses, is receiving the second level of punishment, but the magnitude of his punishment borders that of the third level of punishment.

What kind of evil did Pharaoh do in this life to deserve this kind of punishment? Why was he sent to the Lower Grave?

When the Israelites were oppressed as slaves, Moses was called on by God to bring His people out of Egypt and lead them into the Promised Land of Canaan. Moses went to Pharaoh and told him to let the Israelites leave Egypt. However, understanding the value of the forced labor of the Israelites, Pharaoh refused to let them go.

Through Moses, God sent down the Ten Plagues to Pharaoh, his officials, and his people. The water in the Nile turned into blood. Frogs, gnats, and flies covered his land. In addition, Pharaoh and his people suffered from the plague on livestock, the plague of boils, hail, locusts, and darkness. Every time they suffered from a plague, Pharaoh promised Moses to let the Israelites leave Egypt, only to prevent further plagues. However, Pharaoh broke his promises and repeatedly hardened his heart, after each time Moses prayed to God and He took deadly plagues away from the land. Pharaoh finally let the Israelites go, only after every firstborn son in Egypt, from the heir to the throne to the firstborn son of the slaves, as well as all the firstborns of the cattle were killed.

However, soon after the last plague, Pharaoh again changed his mind. He and his army began to pursue the Israelites, who were camped by the Red Sea. The Israelites were terrified and cried out to God. Moses raised his staff and stretched out his hand over the Red Sea. Then, a miracle took place. The Red Sea was divided in half by the power of God. The Israelites crossed the Red Sea on dry ground and the Egyptians followed them into the Sea. When Moses stretched out his hand over the sea again on the other side of the Red Sea, *"The waters returned and covered the chariots and the horsemen, even Pharaoh's entire army that had gone into the sea after them; not even one of them remained"* (Exodus 14:28).

In the Bible, many good-natured gentile kings believed in and worshiped God. However, Pharaoh had a hardened mind, even though he had witnessed God's power ten times. As a result, Pharaoh fell into serious disasters such as the death of his heir to the throne, destruction of his army, and destitution of his nation.

Nowadays, people hear of the almighty God and directly witness His power. However, they harden their own hearts the way Pharaoh did. They do not accept Jesus as their personal Savior. Furthermore, they refuse to repent of their sins. What will happen to them if they keep on living the way they do now? Eventually, they will receive the same level of punishments as Pharaoh in the Lower Grave.

What is happening to Pharaoh in the Lower Grave?

Pharaoh confined in wastewater

Pharaoh is confined to a pool of wastewater, filled with stench. His body is fastened up in a pool, so he cannot move. He is not alone but there are other souls confined for similar degree of sins.

The fact that he was a king does not provide him with a better treatment in the Lower Grave. Instead, because he was in the position of power, arrogant, served by others, and lived an abundant life, the messengers of hell mock and torture Pharaoh even more severely.

The pool in which Pharaoh is placed is not simply filled with wastewater. Have you ever seen rotting and polluted bodies of water or sewage? How about harbors where ships dock? Such places are filled with gasoline, trash, and stench. It seems impossible for any life to exist in such an environment. If you were to dip your hands in it, you are worried your skin will be contaminated by all the disgusting contents in the water.

Pharaoh finds himself in this confinement. In addition, this pool is filled with countless creepy insects. They resemble grubs but are much bigger.

Insects nibble at the softer parts of the body

These insects approach the souls confined in the pool, and begin nibbling at the softer parts of their bodies first. They gnaw on the eyes, and through the eye sockets, the insects enter the skull and begin nibbling at the brain itself. Can you imagine how painful this is? In the end, they nibble at everything from head to toe. To what can we compare this agony?

How painful is it when dust gets in your eyes? How much more painful will it be when insects nibble at your eyes? Do you believe you can endure the pain when these insects dig up all throughout your body?

Now, suppose a needle is slid underneath your fingernails or pierces your fingertips. These insects continue to peel off the skin and slowly scrape muscles until bones are exposed. These insects do not stop at the back of your hands. They quickly move up to your arms and shoulder and down to your chest, abdomen, legs, and buttocks. The confined souls bear the torture and the pain that accompanies it.

Insects repeatedly nibble at internal organs

Most women, when they see grubs, are frightened by them, much less want to touch them. Imagine, now, much creepier insects much bigger than grubs stinging condemned souls. First, insects pierce their bodies up through their abdomen. Next, they start gnawing on their flesh from the five viscera and the six entrails. The insects then suck the fluids from their brains. During the whole time, condemned souls cannot fight them off, move around, or run away from these dreadful

83

insects.

Insects continue to nibble at their bodies little by little, as the souls watch their body parts being picked at and gnawed on. If we get this kind of torture just for ten minutes, we will go mad. One of such condemned souls in this wretched place is Pharaoh, who challenged God and His servant Moses. He suffers from this agonizing pain while he is fully awake, vividly witnessing and feeling his body parts gnawed on and scraped.

After insects nibbled away at one's body, is that the end of the torture? No. In a little while, the scraped and nibbled parts of one's body are fully restored, and the insects rush back to the soul, gnawing on various body parts. There is no stopping or end to this. Pain does not diminish and he does not get used – therefore become numb – to the torture.

This is how the spiritual world works. In Heaven, if children of God eat fruit from a tree, that fruit is restored. Similarly, in the Lower Grave, regardless of how many times or how much these insects nibble at your body parts, every part of your body is restored immediately after it was shattered and disintegrated.

Even if one led an honest and conscious life

Among honest people are those who do not want or choose to accept Jesus and the gospel. On the outside, they seem good and noble, but they are not good and noble according to the truth.

Galatians 2:16 reminds us to *"know that a man is not justified by observing the law, but by faith in Jesus Christ. So we, too, have put our faith in Christ Jesus that we may be justified by faith in Christ and not by observing the law, because by observing the law, no one will be justified."* A righteous man is the one who can be saved because of the name of Jesus Christ. Only then, can all his sins be forgiven through his faith in Jesus Christ. Moreover, if he believes in Jesus Christ, he will certainly obey the Word of God.

Despite abundant evidences of God's creation of the universe and His wonders and power demonstrated through His servants, if one still denies the almighty God, he is nothing but an evil man with a hard conscience.

From his own perspective, he may have lived an honest life. However, if he keeps on denying Jesus as his personal Savior, he has nowhere to go except Hell. Yet, because such individuals have led comparatively good and honest lives than the wicked who committed sins as much as they wanted following their sinful desires, they will receive either the first or second level of punishments in the Lower Grave.

Among those who die without having an opportunity even to embrace the gospel, if they fail to pass the judgment of conscience, most of them receive the first or second level of punishment. And, a soul receiving the third or fourth level of punishment in the Lower Grave, you can assume, must have been much more wicked and evil than many others.

The Third Level of Punishment

The third and fourth levels of punishments are reserved for all those who turned against God, had their consciences branded, slandered and blasphemed the Holy Spirit, and interfered with the establishment and expansion of the kingdom of God. Furthermore, anyone who has deemed God's churches "heretics" without solid proof also receives the third or fourth level of punishment.

Before delving into the third level of punishment in the Lower Grave, let us briefly examine various forms of tortures man has conceived.

Cruel manmade tortures

During the time when human rights were more of a fantasy than an everyday affair, countless kinds of corporal punishments, including various forms of torture and execution, were devised and carried out.

For instance, in the Middle-Age Europe, prison guards took a prisoner to the basement of the building in order to obtain the confession. Along the way, the prisoner saw bloodstains on the floor and in the room saw different kinds of instruments used and prepared for torture. He heard unbearable shrieks ringing throughout the building, which overwhelmed him.

One of the most common methods of torture was to put the prisoner (or anyone else about to be tortured)'s fingers and toes into tiny metal frames. The metal frames were tightened up until his fingers and toes were crushed. Then, his finger- or toenail was pulled out one by one as the metal frame was tightened up little by little.

If the prisoner made no confession after this, he was then hung in the air with his arms bent backwards and his body twisted in all directions. In this torment, additional pain was inflicted, as his body was lifted up in the air and dropped down to the ground at varying paces. At worst, a heavy piece of iron was tied to the ankle of the prisoner, while he is still hanging in the air. The weight of the iron was sufficient to split all the muscles and bones within his body. If the prisoner still did not make a confession, more horrible and excruciating methods of torture were applied.

The prisoner would be seated in a chair especially designed for torture. On the seat, the back, and the legs of the chair were densely planted tiny gimlets. Upon seeing this frightening object, the prisoner tried to run for his life but prison guards much larger and stronger than him forced him back to the chair. In an instance, the prisoner felt the gimlets piercing his body.

Another kind of torture was to hang a suspect or prisoner upside down. After an hour, his blood pressure went off the chart, blood vessels in the brain burst out, and the blood gushed out of his brain through his eyes, nose, and ears. He could no longer see, smell, or hear.

Sometimes, fire was used to force the prisoner into submission. The official would approach a suspect with a burning candle. He would bring the candle to the suspect's armpits or soles. Armpits are burned because they are one of the most sensitive parts of human bodies while soles are burned because the pain lasts longer there.

Other times, a suspect was forced to wear heated iron boots in bare feet. Then, the torturer plucked out the tender flesh. Or, the torturer would cut off the prisoner's tongue or burn his palate with hot iron tongs. If the prisoner was sentenced to death, he was thrown into the wheel-like frame, which was designed to shatter a body into pieces. The fast spinning ripped the body into pieces, while the prisoner was still alive and conscious. On occasion, they were put to death by having melted lead poured into his nostrils and ear holes.

Knowing that they would not be able to endure the agony

of the torture, many prisoners often bribed torturers and prison guards for a quick and painless death.

These are some of the torture methods devised by man. A mere imagination is enough to leave us frightened at the mental image. Then, you can already presume that tortures carried out by the messengers of hell, who are under the strict leadership of Lucifer, can only be much more agonizing than any other forms of torture that has ever been devised by man. These messengers of hell lack compassion and are only delighted to hear souls scream and cry in terror in the Lower Grave. They are always trying to figure out the crueler and more painful techniques of torture to inflict upon these souls.

Can you afford to go to Hell? Can you afford to see your loved ones, your family and friends in Hell? All Christians must consider it their duty to spread and preach the gospel and do all they can to save one additional soul from falling into Hell.

What, then, exactly are the third level of punishments?

i) A ghastly pig-shaped messenger of hell

One soul in the Lower Grave is tied to a tree, and his flesh is cut into tiny pieces little by little. Perhaps you can compare this to slicing the fish in order to prepare sashimi. A messenger of hell in an ugly and frightening appearances prepares all the necessary tools for the torture. These devices include a wide variety of tools from a small dagger to an ax. Then the messenger of hell whets the tools on a stone. The tools do not need to be sharpened because the edge of each tool in the Lower Grave always remains as sharp as it can be. The real purpose of whetting is to further scare the soul awaiting his torture.

Cutting off the flesh beginning with fingertips

When the soul hears these tools clash and when the messenger of hell approaches him with a creepy grin, how frightened and appalled he must be!

'That knife is about to slice away my flesh...
That ax will soon cut out my limbs...
What am I to do?
How am I to endure the pain?'

The horror alone nearly suffocates him. The soul keeps on reminding himself that he is tightly tied to the trunk of a tree, cannot move, and that it feels like the rope is piercing his body. The more he tries to escape from the tree, the tighter the rope fastens around his body. The messenger of hell approaches him and begins to slice his flesh, starting at his fingertip. A lump of flesh covered with blood clots falls to the ground. The nails of his fingers are plucked out and in a little while, the fingers will be cut off as well. The messenger cuts out his flesh from his fingers, to his wrist, and to his shoulder. All there will be left to his arm are bones. Then the messenger moves down to the soul's calf and the inner thighs.

Until the internal organs are exposed

A messenger of hell begins to cut out his abdomen. When the five viscera and the six entrails are exposed, he snatches those organs and throws them away. He takes and rips other organs with his sharp tools as well.

Up until this point, the soul has been awake and watching the whole process: his flesh cut out and his intestines thrown out. Imagine that someone has tied you up, cuts off a portion of your body starting at the back of your hands, piece by piece, each size about the size of your fingernail. When the knife touches you, the blood is immediately shed and the suffering instantly begins, and no words can adequately express your fear. In the Lower Grave, when you receive this third level of punishment, it is not just a piece of your body; it is the skin of your body in entirety, from head to toe, and all your intestines pulled out, one by one.

Again picture *sashimi,* a Japanese dish of a raw fish. The cook has merely separated its bones and skin. And he sliced its flesh as thinly as possible. The dish is arranged in the form of a live fish. The fish seems to be still alive and you can see its gill move. The cook in the restaurant does not have compassion for the fish because if he did, he could not do his job.

Please keep your parents, your spouse, your relatives, and your friends in prayer. If they are not saved and end up in Hell, they are to suffer from the torment of having their skin cut out and their bones scraped by the merciless messengers of hell. It is our duty as Christians to spread the good news, because on the Day of Judgment, God will surely hold each of us accountable for anyone we could not bring along to Heaven.

Stabbing the soul's eye

The messenger of hell picks up a gimlet instead of a knife this time. The soul already knows what is about to happen to him because it is not the first time he will endure from this; he has already been tortured this way hundreds and thousands of times from the day he has been brought down to the Lower Grave. The messenger of hell approaches the soul, deeply stabs his eye with a gimlet, and leaves the gimlet in the eye socket for a moment. How frightened must the soul be when he sees the gimlet approach him closer and closer? The agony from having a gimlet pierced into his eye is not describable with words.

Is this the end of the torture? No. The soul's face remains. The messenger of hell now cuts out cheeks, the nose, the forehead, and the rest of the face. He does not forget to cut out the skin from the soul's ears, lips, and neck. The neck, as it is carved out little by little, becomes thinner and thinner until it snaps off from the upper torso. This concludes one session of torture, but this end only signifies the beginning of a new round of torture.

One cannot even shriek or cry

In a little while, the parts of his body that were cut out are restored, as if nothing had ever happened to them. While the body regenerates itself, there is a brief moment during which the pain and agony cease to exist. However, this break only reminds the soul of more tortures that await him, and he soon begins to tremble in uncontrollable fear. While he is awaiting the torture, the sound of whetting is heard again. From time to time, a pig-shaped messenger of hell glances at him with a creepy grin. The messenger is ready for a new round of torture. Agonizing torments start all over again. Do you think you can bear this? No parts of your body will ever grow numb to instruments of torture or the continuous pain. The more you are tortured, the more you will suffer.

A suspect in custody or a prisoner about to be tortured knows that what awaits him will only last a short time, but he still trembles and shivers from an overwhelming fear. Suppose, then, an ugly pig-shaped messenger of hell approaching you with various tools in his hands, clashing one against another. The torture will be repeated without an end: slicing away of the flesh, pulling out of the internal organs, piercing into the eyes, and many other will continue.

Therefore, a soul in the Lower Grave cannot scream or beg the messenger of hell for life, mercy, lesser cruelty, or anything else. The shrieking of other souls, cries for mercy, and the clashing of instruments of torture surround the soul. As soon as the soul sees a messenger of hell, he turns pale as ashes without a murmur. Furthermore, he already knows that he cannot free himself from the suffering until he is to be thrown into the lake of fire after the Judgment of the Great White Throne at the end of the age (Revelation 20:11). The grim reality only adds to the pain already existent.

ii) The punishment of inflating the body like a balloon

Anyone with even a bit of conscience is bound to feel guilty if he/she hurts someone else's feeling. Or, no matter how much an individual may have hated someone else in the past, if the latter's life finds itself in misery today, a sense of pity rises while the feeling of hatred diminishes, at least for a while.

However, if one's conscience has been seared as with a hot iron, the person is completely apathetic to the agony of others, and in order to achieve his own goals he may be willing to commit even the most heinous atrocities.

People treated as trash and rubbish

During World War II in Germany under the Nazi dictatorship, Japan, Italy, and other countries, countless people alive were used as subjects in horrendous and clandestine experiments; these people, in essence, had replaced rats, rabbits, and other commonly used animals.

For instance, in order to find out how a healthy individual would respond, how long he would last against various malicious agents, and what kind of symptoms accompanied various diseases, cancer cells and other viruses were transplanted. To obtain the most accurate information, they often cut open the stomachs or the skull of a live person. To determine how an average person responds to extreme cold or heat, they rapidly decreased the temperature of a room or rapidly increased the temperature of a water container in which the subjects were confined.

After these "subjects" had served their purpose, these people were often left to die in agony. They gave little thought to the preciousness or anguish of these subjects.

How cruel and horrendous must it have been for many prisoners of war or other powerless individuals who became these notorious subjects, watched their body parts sliced into pieces, against their will had their bodies infected with various lethal cells and agents, and literally watched themselves die?

However, souls in the Lower Grave face even crueler methods of punishments than any experiments on living bodies man has ever conceived. As men and women who had been created in God's own image and likeness, but also as ones who have lost their dignity and value, these souls are treated as disposed trash or rubbish in the Lower Grave.

The way we do not pity trash, the messengers of hell do not pity or have compassion on these souls. The messengers of hell do not feel guilty or sorry for them, and no punishment is ever enough.

The bones shatter and the skin bursts

Therefore, the messengers of hell see these souls merely as playthings. They would inflate the bodies of the souls and kick the bodies around with one another.

It is hard to imagine this sight: How can a long and flat body of a human being be inflated like a ball? What would happen to the organs within?

As the internal organs and the lungs are inflated, ribs and spines protecting these organs are shattered one by one, part by part. On top of this is the constant, excruciating pain from the stretched skin.

The messengers of hell play with these inflated bodies of unsaved souls in the Lower Grave, and when they grow bored of them, they burst the stomachs of the souls with sharp spears. The way a once-inflated balloon is torn into rubber pieces when it is popped, their blood and pieces of skin are shredded into all directions.

However, in a short while, these souls' bodies are wholly restored and placed yet again to the initial place of punishment. How cruel is this? While they lived on this earth, these souls were loved by others, enjoyed some kind of social status, or at least could claim fundamental human rights.

Once in the Lower Grave, however, they have no rights to claim and are treated merely like gravels on the ground; their existence has no value.

Ecclesiastes 12:13-14 reminds us as follows:

The conclusion, when all has been heard, is: fear God and keep His commandments, because this applies to every person. For God will bring every act to judgment, everything which is hidden, whether it is good or evil.

As such, according to His judgment, these souls have been degraded to mere playthings with which the messengers of hell play.

Therefore, we must be aware that if we fail to carry out the duty of man, which is to fear God and keep all His commandments, we will no longer be recognized as precious souls bearing God's own image and likeness, but instead be subject to the cruelest punishments in the Lower Grave.

Punishment on Pontius Pilate

At the time of Jesus' death, Pontius Pilate was a Roman governor in the region of Judea, today Palestine. From the day he set his foot in the Lower Grave, he has been receiving the third level of punishment, which entails whipping, for what specific reasons is Pontius Pilate being tormented?

Despite knowing of Jesus' righteousness

Since Pilate was the governor of Judea, his permission was

required to crucify Jesus. As a Roman viceroy, Pilate was in charge of overseeing the entire region of Judea, and he had many spies at various locations throughout the region working for him. Thus, Pilate was well aware of countless miracles Jesus had performed, His message of love, His healing of the sick, His preaching of God, and the like, as Jesus preached the gospel throughout the region both He and Pilate inhabited. In addition, from the reports his spies had submitted, Pilate concluded Jesus to be a good and innocent man.

Furthermore, because Pilate was aware that the Jews were desperate to kill Jesus out of jealousy, he made every effort to set Him free. However, because Pilate was also convinced that not heeding the Jews would result in a major social unrest in his province, he ended up handing Jesus over to be crucified at the request of the Jews. If unrest had broken out within his jurisdiction, heavy responsibility would have surely threatened Pilate's own life.

In the end, Pilate's cowardly conscience determined his destination after death. The way Roman soldiers flogged Jesus at Pilate's command before His crucifixion, Pilate, too, has been condemned to the same punishment: endless flogging by the messengers of hell.

Pilate flogged every time his name is called

This is how Jesus was flogged. The whip consisted of pieces of iron or bones planted at the end of a long leather strap. At each stroke, the whip would wrap Jesus' body, and the bones and metal pieces at the end of it would pierce His flesh. At a snatch, the flesh was stripped from the wounds, which the whip had struck, leaving behind big and deep gashes.

Likewise, whenever people call out his name in this world, the messengers of hell flog Pilate in the Lower Grave. During each worship service, many Christians recite the Apostles' Creed. Whenever the part "suffered under Pontius Pilate" is recited, he is whipped. When hundreds and thousands of people recite his name together at the same time, the rate at which he is flogged and the strength of each whip increase dramatically. At times, other messengers of hell gather around Pilate to offer each other a hand in flogging him.

Although Pilate's body has been torn into pieces and is covered with blood, the messengers of hell flog him as if they were competing against each other. The flogging tears up Pilate's flesh, exposes his bones, and digs up his medullae.

His tongue is permanently removed

While he is tortured, Pilate is constantly shouting out, "Please don't call out my name! Each time it is called, I suffer and suffer." However, not a sound is heard from his mouth. His tongue has been cut off, because with the same tongue he sentenced Jesus to be crucified. When you are in pain, it helps a little to scream and shriek. For Pilate, not even such an option is available.

There is something different with Pilate. For other condemned souls in the Lower Grave, when various body parts are scraped, cut off, or burned, those body parts regenerate themselves. However, Pilate's tongue has been permanently removed as the symbol of a curse. Even though Pilate begs and begs people not to call on his name, it will be recited until the Judgment Day. The more his name is called, the heavier his suffering becomes.

Pilate deliberately committed a sin

When Pilate handed Jesus over to be crucified, he took water and washed his hands in front of the crowd, and then said to the people, *"I am innocent of this Man's blood; see to that yourselves"* (Matthew 27:24). In response, the Jews, now more desperate than ever to have Jesus killed, answered Pilate, *"His blood shall be on us and on our children!"* (Matthew 27:25).

What happened to the Jews after Jesus was crucified? They were massacred when the city of Jerusalem was captured and destroyed by the Roman General Titus in 70 A.D. Since then, they were scattered all over the world and oppressed in lands not their own. During World War II, they were forcibly relocated to numerous concentration camps in Europe, where over six million Jews were suffocated to death in gas chambers or otherwise brutally massacred. During the first five decades of its modern statehood after the 1948 independence, the state of Israel has constantly faced threats, hatred, and armed opposition from its neighbors in the Middle East.

Even though the Jews have received retribution for their demand "His blood shall be on us and on our children!" this does not mean the punishment for Pilate has in any way been reduced. Pilate deliberately committed a sin. He had plenty of opportunities not to commit the sin, but he did anyway. Even his wife, after having been warned in a dream, urged Pilate not to have Jesus killed. Ignoring his own conscience and the advice of his wife, Pilate nevertheless sentenced Jesus to be crucified. As a result, he was forced to receive the third level of punishment in the Lower Grave.

Even today, people commit crimes even if they know they are crimes. They expose secrets of some to others for their own benefits. In the Lower Grave, the third level of punishment is inflicted upon those who plot against others, give false testimony, slander, form factions or gangs to murder or torture, act cowardly, betray others in times of danger or pain, and the like.

God will bring every deed into question

Just as Pilate placed the blood of Jesus in the hands of the Jews by washing his hands, some people place blame for a particular situation or condition on other people. However, responsibility for people's sins rest on themselves. Each individual has a free will, and he not only has the right to make decisions, but he will also be held accountable for his decisions. Free will allows us to make a choice between whether or not to believe Jesus as our personal Savior, whether or not we should keep the Lord's Day holy, whether or not we should offer the whole tithe to God, and the like. However, the result of our choice is revealed through either the eternal happiness in Heaven or the eternal punishment in Hell.

Moreover, the result of any decision you have ever made is your own to bear, so you cannot blame anyone else for it. That is why you cannot say things like "I left God because of my parents' persecution" or "I could not keep the Lord's Day holy or give my whole tithe to God because of my spouse." If one had had faith, the individual would surely have feared God and kept all His commandments.

Pilate, whose tongue has been cut off because of his own cowardly words, has been remorseful and regretting while being constantly flogged in the Lower Grave. After death, however, there is no second chance for Pilate.

However, those who are alive still have a chance. You should never hesitate to fear God and keep His commandments. Isaiah 55:6-7 tells us, *"Seek the LORD while He may be found; call upon Him while He is near. Let the wicked forsake his way and the unrighteous man his thoughts; and let him return to the LORD, and He will have compassion on him, and to our God, for He will abundantly pardon."* Because God is love, He allows us to know what is happening in Hell while we are still alive. He does so to awaken many people from their spiritual slumber, and empower and encourage us to spread the good news to even more people so that they, too, may live in His mercy and compassion.

Punishment on Saul the First King of Israel

Jeremiah 29:11 tells us that *" 'For I know the plans that I have for you,' declares the LORD, 'plans for welfare and not for calamity to give you a future and a hope.'"* The Word was given to the Jews when they were exiled to Babylon. The verse prophesies God's forgiveness and mercy that will be granted to His people, when they are in exile because of their sins against their God.

For the same reason, God is declaring the messages on Hell. He does so not to curse the nonbelievers and sinners, but to redeem all those carrying a heavy burden as slaves to the enemy Satan and the devil, and prevent people created in His image from falling to that wretched place.

Thus, instead of fearing the miserable conditions of Hell, all we have to do now is to understand the immeasurable love of God and, if you are a nonbeliever, accept Jesus Christ as your personal Savior from this point on. If you have not lived according to the Word of God professing your faith in Him, turn around and do as He tells you.

Saul remained disobedient to God

When Saul ascended to the throne, he greatly humbled himself. However, he soon became too arrogant to obey the Word of God. He fell into the evil ways to be abandoned and in the end, God turned His face away from Saul. When you sin against God, you must alter your mindset and repent without hesitation. You should not try to excuse yourself or hide your sin. Only then, will God receive your prayer of repentance and open the way of forgiveness.

When Saul learned that God had anointed David to replace him, the king deemed his successor-to-be his nemesis and sought to kill him for the rest of his life. Saul even killed the priests of God for helping David (1 Samuel 22:18). Such deeds were the same as confronting God, face to face.

In this way, King Saul remained disobedient and amassed his evil deeds but God did not destroy Saul immediately. Even though Saul was after David and determined to kill him for a very long time, God continued to let Saul live.

This served two purposes. One, God intended to mold a great vessel and king out of David. Two, God gave Saul enough time and opportunities to repent of his wrongdoings.

If God had killed us when we committed a sin grave enough to be put to death, none of us would have survived. God will forgive, wait, and wait, but if one does not return to Him, God will look the other way. However, Saul could not understand the heart of God and pursued the desire of the flesh. In the end, Saul was critically wounded by archers and then killed himself with his own sword (1 Samuel 31:3-4).

Saul's body is hanging in the air

What is the punishment for the arrogant Saul? A sharp spear is piercing his abdomen as he is hanging in the air. The blade of the spear is densely planted with objects that resemble sharp gimlets and edges of a sword.

It is tremendously painful to be hung in the air as it is. It is even more excruciating to be hung in the air while a spear is piercing through your abdomen, and your weight only adds to the pain. The spear shreds the pierced abdomen apart with sharp blades and gimlets. As the skin is torn apart, muscles, bones, and intestines are exposed.

When, at times, the messenger of hell approaches Saul and turns the spear, all the sharp blades and gimlets attached to it also tear up the body. This spinning of the spear bursts Saul's lungs, heart, stomach, and intestines.

A short while after Saul endures this awful torture and his intestines shredded into pieces, all his internal organs are fully restored. Once they are fully restored, the messenger of hell approaches Saul and repeats the procedure. As he suffers, Saul will reflect on all the times and opportunities of repentance he ignored in this life.

Why did I disobey the will of God?
Why did I fight against Him?
I should have paid attention to
Prophet Samuel's rebuke!

I should have repented
when my son Jonathan pleaded with me in tears!
Only if I had not been so evil towards David,
my punishment might have been lighter...

It is useless for Saul to be remorseful or repent after he has fallen into Hell. It is unbearable to be hung in the air with a spear piercing his abdomen, but when the messenger of hell approaches Saul for another round of torture, Saul is overwhelmed with fear. Pain endured from only moments before are still all too real and vivid for him, and he almost suffocates at the thought of things to come.

Saul may beg, "Please leave me alone!" or "Please, stop this torture!" but it is useless. The more scared Saul becomes, the more delighted the messenger of hell becomes. He will turn and turn the spear, and the agony of having his body torn apart is repeated perpetually for Saul.

Arrogance is the spearhead of destruction

The following case is a commonplace in any church today. A new believer, at first, will receive and be filled with the Holy Spirit. He will be eager to serve God and His servants for a little while. However, that believer will begin to disobey the will of God, His church, and His servants. If this adds up, he will begin to judge and condemn others with the Word of God he has heard. He will also be very likely to become arrogant in deed.

The first love he shared with the Lord has gradually diminished over time, and his hope – once placed in Heaven – is now with things of this world – things he once abandoned.

103

Even in the church, he now wants to be served by others, becomes greedy for money and power, and indulges in the desire of the flesh.

When he was poor, he might have prayed, "God, give me the blessing of material fortune!" What happens once he does receive the blessing? Instead of using the blessing in helping the poor, missionaries, and God's works, he now wastes God's blessing on pursuing pleasures of this world.

For this, the Holy Spirit within the believer laments; his spirit faces many trials and difficulties; and punishment may be on the way. If he keeps on sinning, his conscience may become numb. He may become unable to distinguish God's will from the greed of his heart, often pursuing the latter.

Sometimes, he may become jealous of God's servants who are greatly admired and loved by the members of their church. He may falsely incriminate them and interfere with their ministries. For his own benefits, he creates factions within the church, thereby destroying the church in which the Christ dwells.

Such person will continue to confront God and become the tool of the enemy Satan and the devil, and in the end resemble Saul.

God opposes the proud but gives grace to the humble

1 Peter 5:5 reads that *"You younger men, likewise, be subject to your elders; and all of you, clothe yourselves with humility toward one another, for God is opposed to the proud, but gives grace to the humble."* The proud judge the message preached from the podium while they hear it. They accept what agrees with their own thoughts, but reject what does not agree. Most

human thoughts are different from God's. You cannot say you believe and love God if you accept only the things that match your thoughts.

1 John 2:15 tells us, *"Do not love the world nor the things in the world. If anyone loves the world, the love of the Father is not in him."* Likewise, if the love of Father is not with that individual, he or she does not have a fellowship with God. That is why, if you claim to have a fellowship with Him yet still walk in the darkness, you lie and do not live by the truth (1 John 1:6).

You should always be careful and constantly examine yourself to see whether you might have become arrogant, whether you want to be served instead of serving others, and whether the love for this world has crept in your heart.

The Fourth Level of Punishment on Judas Iscariot

We have seen that the first, second, and third levels of punishments in the Lower Grave are so miserable and cruel beyond our imagination. We have also examined numerous reasons these souls receive such cruel punishments.

From this point on, let us delve into the most frightening punishments of all in the Lower Grave. What are some examples of the fourth level of punishments and what kind of evil have these souls committed to deserve them?

Committing an unforgivable sin

The Bible tells us that for some sins you may be forgiven

through repentance, while there are other kinds of sins for which you cannot be forgiven, the kind of sins that lead you to death (Matthew 12:31-32; Hebrew 6:4-6; 1 John 5:16). People who blaspheme the Holy Spirit, purposely commit a sin while knowing the truth, and the like apply to this category of sins, and they will fall into the deepest part of the Lower Grave.

For instance, we often see people who have been healed or had their problems resolved through the grace of God. At first, they are enthusiastic to work for God and His church. However, at times we see them tempted by the world, and eventually turn their backs on God.

They indulge in the pleasure of this world again, only this time, they do so much more than before. They subject churches to disgrace and insult other Christians and God's servants. Oftentimes, those publicly professing their faith in God are the first to judge and label churches or pastors as "heretics" based on their own perspectives and reasoning. When they see a church filled with the power of the Holy Spirit and God's miracles working through His servants, simply because they are unable to comprehend, they are quick to judge the entire congregation as "heretics" or consider the works of the Holy Spirit as those of Satan.

They have betrayed God and cannot receive the spirit of repentance. In other words, such people will not be able to repent of their sins. Thus, after death, these "Christians" will receive heavier punishments than those who did not believe Jesus Christ as their personal Savior and ended up in the Lower Grave.

2 Peter 2:20-21 tells us that *"For if, after they have escaped the defilements of the world by the knowledge of the Lord and Savior Jesus Christ, they are again entangled in them and are*

overcome, the last state has become worse for them than the first. For it would be better for them not to have known the way of righteousness, than having known it, to turn away from the holy commandment handed on to them." These people disobeyed the Word of God and challenged Him even if they had known the Word and for this, they will receive punishments far greater and heavier than the ones who did not believe.

People whose consciences are branded

Souls receiving the fourth level of punishments have not only committed unforgivable sins, but also had their consciences branded. Some of these people have wholly become slaves to the enemy Satan and the devil, who confronted God and ruthlessly opposed the Holy Spirit. It is as if they crucified Jesus on the cross in person.

Jesus our Savior was crucified to forgive our sins and free man from the curse of the eternal death. His precious blood redeemed all those who believed in Him, but the curse on people receiving the fourth level of punishments makes them ineligible to receive salvation even with the blood of Jesus Christ. Hence, they have been doomed to be crucified on their own crosses and receive their own punishments in the Lower Grave.

Judas Iscariot, one of Jesus' Twelve Disciples and perhaps the best-known traitor in the history of mankind, is a prime example. With his own eyes, Judas saw the Son of God in flesh. He became one of Jesus' disciples, learned the Word, and witnessed miraculous works and signs. Yet, Judas was never able to throw away his greed and sin to the end. Finally, Judas was instigated by Satan and sold his teacher for 30 pieces of silver.

No matter how much Judas Iscariot wanted to repent

Who do you think is guiltier: Pontius Pilate who sentenced Jesus to be crucified, or Judas Iscariot who sold Jesus over to the Jews? Jesus' response to one of Pilate's questions provides us with a clear answer:

You would have no authority over Me, unless it had been given you from above; for this reason he who delivered Me to you has the greater sin (John 19:11).

The sin Judas committed is truly a greater sin, one for which he cannot be forgiven and is not given a spirit of repentance. When Judas realized the magnitude of his sin, he regretted and returned the money, but he was never given a spirit of repentance.

In the end, unable to overcome the burden of his sin, in anguish Judas Iscariot committed suicide. Acts 1:18 tells us that Judas *"acquired a field with the price of his wickedness, and falling headlong, he burst open in the middle and all his intestines gushed out,"* describing his miserable end.

Judas hung on a cross

What kind of punishment is Judas receiving in the Lower Grave? In the deepest part of the Lower Grave, Judas is hung on a cross on the forefront. With Judas and his cross on the forefront, crosses of those who had severely confronted God are lined up. The scene resembles a mass grave or a cemetery after a full-scale war or a slaughterhouse filled with dead livestock.

Crucifixion is one of the cruelest punishments even in this world. The use of crucifixion serves as an example as well as a warning to all the criminals and criminals-to-be of their possible future. Anyone hanging on a cross, which is an agony greater than death itself, for a number of hours – during which body parts are torn into pieces, insects nibble at the body, and all blood gushes out of his body – anxiously longs to draw his last breath as quickly as possible.

In this world, the pain of crucifixion lasts at most half a day. However, in the Lower Grave where there is no end to torture and certainly no death, the tragedy of the punishment by crucifixion will continue until the Judgment Day.

Furthermore, Judas is wearing a crown made of thorns, which continuously grow and rip his skin, pierce the skull, and transfix the brain. In addition, beneath his feet are what appear to be squirming animals. A closer look reveals them as other souls who have fallen into the Lower Grave, and even these are tormenting Judas. In this world, they also confronted God and amassed evil, as their conscience was branded. They, too, are receiving harsh punishments and tortures, and the more severe torture they receive, the more violent they become. In turn, as if to vent out their anger and agony, they keep on stabbing Judas with spears.

Then, the messengers of hell mock Judas, saying, "This is the one who sold the Messiah! He has made things good for us! Good for him! How ridiculous!"

Great mental torment for having sold the Son of God

In the Lower Grave, Judas Iscariot has to endure not only

the physical torture, but also an unbearable amount of mental torment. He will always remember that he was cursed for having sold the Son of God. In addition, because the name "Judas Iscariot" has become synonymous with betrayal even in this world, his mental torment increases accordingly.

Jesus knew in advance that Judas would betray Him and what would happen to Judas after death. That is why Jesus tried to win Judas back with the Word, but He also knew that Judas would not be won back. Thus, in Mark 14:21, we find Jesus lamenting, *"For the Son of Man is to go just as it is written of Him; but woe to that man by whom the Son of Man is betrayed! It would have been good for that man if he had not been born."*

In other words, if an individual receives the first level of punishment, which is the lightest punishment, it would be better for him not to be born at all because the pain is so great and tremendous. What about Judas? He is receiving the heaviest of punishments!

In order not to fall into Hell

Who, then, fears God and keeps His commandments? It is the one who always keeps the Lord's Day holy and gives the whole tithe to God – the two fundamental elements of life in Christ.

Keeping the Lord's Day holy symbolizes your recognition of God's sovereignty of the spiritual realm. Keeping the Lord's Day holy serves as a sign that recognizes and distinguishes you as one of God's children. If you do not keep the Lord's Day holy, however, no matter how much you confess your faith in Father God, there is no spiritual verification of your being one of God's children. In such a case, you have no other choice but to go to Hell.

Giving the whole tithe to God means that you acknowledge God's sovereignty over property. It also means that you recognize and understand that God's sole ownership of the entire universe. According to Malachi 3:9, Israelites were cursed after "robbing [God]." He created the entire universe and gave a life to you. He gives us the sunlight and the rainfall to live, the energy to work, and the protection to guard a day's work. God owns all you have. Thus, even though all our incomes do belong to God, He allowed us to give Him only a tenth of whatever we earn, and use the rest at our disposal. The LORD of hosts says in Malachi 3:10, *"Bring the whole tithe into the storehouse, so that there may be food in My house, and test Me now in this, if I will not open for you the windows of Heaven and pour out for you a blessing until it overflows."* So long as we remain faithful to Him with regard to the tithe, God, as promised, will throw open the floodgates of Heaven and pour out so much blessing that we will not have room enough for it. However, if you do not give the tithe to God, it means that you do not believe in His promise of blessing, lack the faith to be saved, and, since you have robbed God, you have no other place to go but Hell.

Therefore, we must always keep our Lord's Day holy, give the whole tithe to the One to whom everything belongs, and keep His all commandments prescribed in all sixty-six books of the Bible. I pray that none of the readers of this book will fall into Hell.

In this chapter, we delved into various kinds of punishments – divided largely into four levels – that are inflicted upon the condemned souls confined in the Lower Grave. How cruel, frightening, miserable a place is this?

2 Peter 2:9-10 tells us that *"Then the Lord knows how to rescue the godly from temptation, and to keep the unrighteous under punishment for the day of judgment, and especially those who indulge the flesh in its corrupt desires and despise authority. Daring, self-willed, they do not tremble when they revile angelic majesties."*

Evil men committing sins and doing evil, and interfering or disrupting with the works of the church, do not fear God. Such people who blatantly confront God cannot and should not seek or expect to receive God's help in times of affliction and trials. Until the Judgment of the Great White Throne is carried out, they will be confined in the depths of the Lower Grave and receive punishments in accordance with the kinds and magnitudes of their evil deeds.

Those who lead good, righteous, and devoted lives are always obedient to God in faith. Thus, even when man's wickedness filled the earth and God had to open the floodgates of the heavens, we see that only Noah and his family were saved (Genesis 6-8).

The way Noah feared God and obeyed His commandments and thereby avoided the judgment and reached salvation, we, too, must become obedient children of God in everything we do so that we will become God's true children and accomplish His providence.

Chapter 6

Punishments for Blaspheming the Holy Spirit

In Matthew 12:31-32, Jesus tells us, *"Therefore I say to you, any sin and blasphemy shall be forgiven people, but blasphemy against the Spirit shall not be forgiven. Whoever speaks a word against the Son of Man, it shall be forgiven him; but whoever speaks against the Holy Spirit, it shall not be forgiven him, either in this age or in the age to come."*

Jesus uttered these words towards the Jews, who had reproached Him for preaching the gospel and performing the works of divine power, arguing that He was under the spell of the evil spirit or that He was performing the miracles by the power of the enemy Satan and the devil.

Even today, many people who profess their faith in Christ condemn churches that are filled with the powerful works and wonders of the Holy Spirit, and label them as "heretics" or "the devil's work" simply because they are unable to comprehend or accept it. Yet, how else can the kingdom of God be expanded and the gospel spread around the world without the power and authority that comes from God, which is to say, the works of the Holy Spirit?

Opposing the works of the Holy Spirit is no different from

opposing God Himself. God, then, will not recognize those who oppose the works of the Holy Spirit as His children, no matter how much they consider themselves "Christian."

Thus, bear in mind that even after seeing and experiencing God's dwelling with His servants and wonderful and miraculous signs and events taking place, if one still condemns God's servants and His church as "heretical," he has severely obstructed and blasphemed the Holy Spirit and the only place reserved for him is the depths of Hell.

If a church, a pastor, or any other servants of God truly recognize the Triune God, believe the Bible to be the Word of God and teach it as such, are aware of the life to come in either Heaven or Hell and the Judgment, and believe that God has sovereignty over everything and Jesus is our Savior and teach them as such, no one should or can condemn and label the church, the pastor, and the servants of God "heretics."

I founded the Manmin Church in 1982 and have led countless souls to the way of salvation through the works of the Holy Spirit. Amazingly, among the people who themselves had personally experienced the works of the living God were those who actually confronted God by actively obstructing the goals and works of the congregation, and spreading rumors and lies about me and the church.

While explaining the misery and agony of Hell in depth, God also revealed to me about the punishments that await in the Lower Grave those who obstruct, disobey, and blaspheme the Holy Spirit. What kinds of punishments will they receive?

Suffering in a Pot of Boiling Liquid

I regret and curse the marriage vows
I made with my husband.
Why am I in this wretched place?
He deluded me and because of him, I am here!

This is a lamentation of a wife who is receiving the fourth
level of punishment in the Lower Grave. The reason her
agonizing groan is echoing throughout the dark and ashy
expanse is because her husband deluded her to confront God
with him.

The wife was evil yet her heart had, to a certain extent,
feared God. Thus, the woman was not able to obstruct the
Holy Spirit and contend with God on her own. However, in
pursuant to her desires of flesh, her conscience was paired with
her husband's evil conscience, and the couple greatly opposed
God and His works.

The couple who did evil together is now punished together
as a couple even in the Lower Grave, and will suffer for all their
evil deeds. What, then, will entail their punishments in the
Lower Grave?

A couple tormented one by one

The pot is filled with terrible stench and the condemned
souls are dipped in the briskly boiling liquid, one by one. When
a messenger of hell puts each soul into the pot, the temperature
of the liquid blisters the whole body – now much resembling
the back of a toad – and the eyeballs spring out.

Whenever they desperately try to avoid this torment and

stick their heads out of the pot, huge feet trample on and submerge their heads. Planted densely on the soles of these huge feet of the messengers of hell are tiny iron or brass skewers. When trampled down by these feet, the souls are forced back into the pot with big gashes and bruises.

After a while, the souls stick their heads out again because they cannot endure the burning sensation. Right then, as done many times before, they are trampled and pushed back into the pot. Furthermore, because souls take turns in receiving this torment, if the husband is inside the pot, the wife has to watch his anguish, and vice versa.

This pot is transparent so the inside of the pot is visible to the outside. At first, when the husband or the wife sees his/her loved one tortured and tormented in such a wretched manner, out of mutual affection each cries for mercy on behalf of the other:

My wife is in there!
Please take her out!
Please release her from the misery.
No, no, don't trample on her.
Please take her out, please!

After some time, however, the husband's entreaty ceases. After having been punished a few times, he has come to realize that while his wife suffers, he is able to take a break, and that when she comes out of the pot, it is his turn to enter it.

Blaming and cursing each other

Married couples in this world will not be couples in Heaven. However, this couple will remain as a couple in the Lower

Grave, and receive punishments together. Thus, because they know they should take turns in receiving their punishments, their entreaties now carry drastically different tones.

No, no, please don't take her out.
Let her stay in there a little longer.
Please leave her there
so that I can rest a little more.

The wife wants her husband to suffer continuously, and the husband also begs for his wife to stay in the pot as long as possible. However, watching one suffer does not give the other time to rest. Brief breaks do not and cannot make up for lasting agony, especially because the husband knows after his wife, it is his turn. Furthermore, when one is in torment and sees and hears the other pleading for longer punishment, the two curse each other.

Here, we become clearly aware of the result of fleshly love. The reality of fleshly love – and the reality of Hell – is that when one suffers from an unbearable amount and magnitude of torment, he or she readily wishes for the other to be tormented, on his/her own behalf.

As the wife regrets having confronted God "because of her husband," she eagerly tells her husband, "Because of you I am here!" In response, and in a louder voice, the husband curses and blames his wife who supported and participated in his evil deeds.

The more evil the couple commits…

The messengers of hell in the Lower Grave are so joyous and

delighted with this husband and wife who curse each other, and entreat to the messengers that their spouse be punished longer and more severely.

Look, they curse each other even here!
Their evil delights us so much!

As if they were seeing an interesting movie, the messengers of hell pay close attention and every now and then they feed the fire even further to thoroughly enjoy themselves. The more the husband and wife suffer, the more they curse each other and naturally, the messengers' laughter becomes louder.

We have to clearly understand one point here. When people commit evil even in this life, evil spirits are delighted and joyous. At the same time, the more evil people commit, the more estranged they become from God.

When you face difficulties and you compromise with the world, lament, complain, and grow bitter towards specific individuals or circumstances, the enemy devil comes running to you, and happily increases your difficulties and tribulations.

The wise men who know the law of the spiritual world will never lament or complain, but instead give thanks under all circumstances and in positive attitude always confess their faith in God, so that they make sure the focus of their hearts is always on Him. Furthermore, if an evil, evil person should afflict you, as Romans 12:21 tells us *"Do not be overcome by evil, but overcome evil with good,"* you must always face evil only with good and commit your all to God.

Likewise, when you follow what is good and walk in the light, you will possess the power and authority to overcome the influence of evil spirits. Then, the enemy Satan and the devil cannot hold you accountable to be evil and all your difficulties will go away much faster. God is pleased when His children act and live according to their good faith.

Under no circumstances should you emanate evil from within the way our enemy Satan and the devil wants, but always think in truth and behave in faith in a way that is pleasing to our Father God.

Climbing Up a Perpendicular Cliff

Whether you are God's servant, an elder, or a worker in His church, you are one day likely to become prey to Satan if you do not circumcise your heart but keep on sinning. Some people turn away from God because they love the world. Others stop attending church after having been tempted. Still others confront God by obstructing His church's plans and missions, which leaves them helplessly on the path to death.

A case of an entire family betraying God

The following is a story about the family of an individual who had once faithfully worked for God's church. They did not circumcise their hearts, which were filled with hot-temper and greed. Therefore, they wielded their power to other church members and committed sins repeatedly. In the end, God's punishment descended on them, as the father of the family was diagnosed with a serious illness. The entire family came together and began offering prayer of earnest repentance as well as prayer for his life.

God received their prayer of repentance and healed the father. At the time, God told me something completely unexpected: "If I call his spirit now, he may receive at least the shameful salvation. If I let him live a little longer, he will not receive any kind of salvation."

I did not understand what He meant but a few months later, as I witnessed the family's behavior, I soon got to understand it. One member of the family had been a faithful worker at my church. He began to obstruct God's church and His kingdom by falsely testifying against the church and carrying out many other evil deeds. In the end, the entire family became deluded and everyone turned away from God.

When the former worker at my church obstructed and severely blasphemed the Holy Spirit, the rest of the family committed unforgivable sins, and the father who had been revived through my prayer died soon afterwards. If the father had died when he had even the small amount of faith, he could have been saved. However, he forsook his faith, leaving himself no chance for salvation. Furthermore, each member of the family will also fall into the Lower Grave, into which the father fell, and where everyone in the family is to receive punishments. What will their punishment entail?

Climbing up a perpendicular cliff with no rest

In the area where the family is punished, there stands a perpendicular cliff. This cliff stands so tall that its top is not visible from the bottom. Frightening shrills fill the air. About halfway up this bloody cliff are three souls punished, who from a distance look like three small dots.

They are climbing up this rough and hardy cliff in bare

hands and bare feet. As if their hands and feet were rubbed with sandpaper, their skin is quickly peeled off and becomes worn out. Their bodies are drenched in blood. The reason they are climbing up this seemingly impossible cliff is to avoid a messenger of hell who is flying over the area.

When this messenger of hell, after watching these three souls climb up the cliff for a while, raises his hands, tiny insects that exactly look like the messenger of hell are scattered all over the land like particles of water spouted from a spray. Exposing their sharp teeth with their mouths wide open, these insects climb up the cliff quickly and chase the souls.

Imagine seeing hundreds of centipedes, tarantulas, or cockroaches, all of them about the size of a finger, covering the floor when you enter your home. Also, imagine all these frightening insects running towards you, all of them at once.

The sight of such insects alone is enough to frighten you. If all these insects rush toward you at once, it may be the most bloodcurdling moment of your life. If these insects begin climbing up your feet and legs and soon overwhelm your body, how can anyone possibly describe such a horrific scene?

In the Lower Grave, however, it is impossible to tell whether there are hundreds or thousands of these insects. The souls only know that there are an incalculable number of these insects, and that the three are their prey.

Countless insects rush to the three souls

Upon seeing these insects at the bottom of the cliff, the three souls are climbing up the cliff faster and faster. Before long, however, the three souls are immediately caught up, overwhelmed, and they fall to the ground on which they are left by themselves to have all their body parts nibbled at by these horrific insects.

When these souls have their body parts gnawed on, the pain is so great and unbearable that they cry out like beasts and helplessly twist and shake their bodies back and forth. They try to shake the insects off themselves, and do so by trampling and pressing down one another, as they continuously rebuke and curse one another. In the midst of such agony, each one emanates more evil than the other does, and seeks only his/her own self-interests and continues to curse one another. The messengers of hell seem to enjoy this sight more than anything else they have ever seen.

Then, when the messenger of hell hovering over the area holds out his hand and collects these insects, in an instant they all disappear. The three souls do not feel the gnawing of insects now, but they cannot stop climbing up the perpendicular cliff. They are well aware how the flying messenger of hell will unleash the insects again soon. With all their might, they resume climbing up the cliff. In this eerie tranquility, the three souls are caught up in a crushing fear of things to come and struggle to climb up the cliff.

The pain of gashes they get while they are climbing cannot be easily ignored. Still, because the fear of insects nibbling at their bodies and having them shredded is far greater, the three souls overlook their bodies smeared with blood, and climb as fast as they can. How miserable this sight is!

Scorched in the Mouth with a Heated Iron

Proverbs 18:21 tells us that *"Death and life are in the power of the tongue, and those who love it will eat its fruit."* Jesus in Matthew 12:36-37 tells us, *"But I tell you that every careless word that people speak, they shall give an accounting for it in the day of judgment. For by your words you will be justified, and by your words you will be condemned."* The two passages tell us that God will hold our words responsible and judge us accordingly.

On the one hand, those who speak the good words of truth bear good fruit according to their words. On the other hand, those who utter evil words without faith bear the evil fruit according to evil words spoken through their evil lips. We sometimes see how words spoken carelessly can bring forth an unbearable amount and magnitude of pain and anguish.

Every word will be paid back

Some believers, because of persecution of their families, say or pray, "If my family can repent through an accident, it will be worth it." As soon as the enemy Satan and the devil hear these words, they accuse the person to God, saying, "The words of this person ought to be fulfilled." Thus, words do become seeds and the accident, from which people become disabled and face additional difficulties, does end up taking place.

Is there a need to bring suffering upon yourself with such foolish and unnecessary words? Unfortunately, when affliction clouds their lives, many people falter. Others do not even realize that the difficulties have come because of their own words, and still others do not even remember what they spoke to cause such distress.

Therefore, keeping in mind that every word will be paid back one way or another, we must always be on our best behavior and restrain our tongues. Regardless of the intent, if what you speak is anything but good and beautiful, Satan can easily – and certainly will – hold you responsible for your words and you will be subject to agonizing, and sometimes unnecessary, troubles.

What would happen to someone who purposely lies about God's church and His beloved servant, and thereby greatly obstructs the church's missions and confronts God? He or she will quickly be led under Satan's influence and to punishments in Hell.

The following is only an example of punishments inflicted upon all those who obstructed the Holy Spirit with their words.

People opposing the Holy Spirit with words

There was a person who had attended and served my church for a long time, holding many kinds of positions. However, he did not circumcise his heart, which is by far the most important thing required of all Christians. On the outside, he seemed by every measure to be a faithful worker who loved God, the church, and his fellow church members.

Among his family members were someone who had been healed of the incurable disease that could have left him permanently disabled and another who had been revived at the threshold of death. Aside from these, his family had many experiences and blessings from God, but he never ended up circumcising his heart and throwing away evil.

So, when the church as a whole faced serious difficulties, his family members were tempted by Satan to betray it. Not remembering the grace and blessings he had received through the church, he left the church he had long served. Furthermore, he began to oppose this church and soon, as if he were on an evangelization mission, he himself began visiting church members and interfered with their faith.

Even if he had left church because of uncertainty in his faith, he might have had the opportunity to receive God's pity in the end, if he had only kept quiet on matters with which he was not familiar and tried to discern right from wrong.

However, he could not overcome his own evil and sinned too much with his tongue that now, only an agonizing retribution awaits him.

Mouth scorched and body twisted

A messenger of hell scorches his mouth with a heated iron because he severely opposed the Holy Spirit with the words coming out of his mouth. This punishment is similar to that of Pontius Pilate, who sentenced the innocent Jesus to crucifixion with the words out of his mouth, and now has his tongue permanently removed in the Lower Grave.

In addition, the soul is forced to enter a glass tube that has stoppers on either base, where metal handles are placed. When the messengers of hell turn these handles, the body of the entrapped soul is twisted. His body is twisted more and more, and as dirty water is squeezed from a mop, the soul's blood spurts through his eyes, nose, mouth, and all other holes in his body. In the end, all his blood and sap gush out from his cells.

Can you imagine how much force needs to be applied to squeeze a drop of blood by twisting your finger?

The soul's blood and sap are squeezed not just from one part of his body but his entire body, from head to toe. All his bones and muscular systems are twisted and shattered and all his cells disintegrated, so that even the last drop of any kind of liquid from the body can be squeezed. How painful this must be!

Finally, the glass tube is full of blood and sap from his body, so that it looks like a bottle of red wine from a distance. After the messengers of hell twist and twist the soul's body until the very last drop of liquid from the body has been spilt, they leave the body alone for a moment to allow it to be restored.

Yet, even if his body is restored, what hope does this soul have? From the moment his body is restored, the twisting and squeezing of his body is repeated without an end. In other words, the moments between his tortures are only an extension of the torture.

For having hindered the kingdom of God with his tongue, this soul's lips are scorched and as a reward for actively helping with the works of Satan, every ounce of liquid in his body is extracted.

In the spiritual world, a man reaps what he sows, and whatever he has done will be done unto him. Please keep this fact in mind, and do not succumb to evil but only with good words and deeds, live a life that is glorifying to God.

Tremendously Large Torturing Machines

This soul personally experienced the works of the Holy Spirit when he was healed of his disease and weakness. After that, he prayed wholeheartedly in order to circumcise his heart. His life was led and supervised by the Holy Spirit and bore the fruit, he won the praise and the love of church members, and became a minister.

Seized in his own pride

As he won the praise and the love of those around him, he increasingly became arrogant that he could no longer look at himself correctly and unconscientiously stopped circumcising his heart. He had always been a man of hot-temper and jealousy, and instead of throwing these things away, he began judging and condemning all those who were right, and he held grudges against anyone who did not please or agree with him.

Once a man is seized in his own pride and does evil, more evil emanates from him and he no longer restrains himself or wishes to heed anyone's advice. This soul piled up evil upon evil, was caught in Satan's snare, and openly opposed God.

Salvation is not complete when we receive the Holy Spirit. Even if you are filled with the Holy Spirit, experience grace, and are serving God, you are like a marathon runner who is still a long way off from the finish line – purification. No matter how well the runner runs, if he or she stops the race or passes out, it does the runner no good. Many people are running toward the finish line – Heaven. No matter how fast you may have run up to a certain point, no matter how close you may have gotten to the finish line, if you stop the race, that is the end of the race for you.

Do not assume you are standing firm

God also tells us that if we are "lukewarm," we will be forsaken (Revelation 3:16). Even if you are a man/woman of faith, you must always be filled with the Holy Spirit; maintain passion for God; and ardently encroach the kingdom of Heaven. If you stop your race halfway through, like the ones who do not participate in the race from the beginning, you cannot be saved.

For that reason, the apostle Paul, who was faithful to God with his whole heart, confessed that *"I affirm, brethren, by the boasting in you which I have in Christ Jesus our Lord, I die daily"* (1 Corinthians 15:31) and that *"I discipline my body and make it my slave, so that, after I have preached to others, I myself will not be disqualified"* (1 Corinthians 9:27).

Even if you are in the position to teach others, if you do not cast off your own thoughts and beat your body to make it your slave the way Paul did, God will forsake you. This is because *"your adversary, the devil, prowls around like a roaring lion, seeking someone to devour"* (1 Peter 5:8).

1 Corinthians 10:12 reads, *"Therefore let him who thinks he stands take heed that he does not fall."* The spiritual world is endless and our becoming more and more like God also knows no end, either. The way a farmer sows seeds in the spring, cultivates throughout the summer, and harvests his crops in the fall, you have to constantly advance in order to make your soul excel and be prepared for meeting the Lord Jesus.

Twisting and picking head

What kinds of punishments await this soul, who stopped circumcising his heart because he thought he was standing firm, yet eventually fell down?

A machine that resembles the messenger of hell, a fallen angel, tortures him. The machine is several times bigger than the messenger of hell is, and gives the soul a chill just to look at it. On the hands of the torturing machine are sharp and pointed fingernails longer than the height of an average human being.

This big torturing machine holds up the soul by his neck with its right hand and twists the soul's head with its left hand's fingernails, which pick his head and dig into his brain. Can you possibly imagine how painful this must be?

This physical pain is tremendous; the mental agony is more unbearable. Before the eyes of the soul is sort of a slideshow that vividly features his happiest moments in this life: happiness felt when he first experienced God's grace, happily praising Him, time when he was eager to fulfill Jesus' command to "go and make disciples of all nations," and the like.

Mental torment and mockery

For the soul, each scene is a dagger to his heart. He was once a servant of the almighty God and was full of the hope for residing in the glorious New Jerusalem. Now, he is confined in this wretched place. This stark contrast tears his heart into pieces. The soul can no longer endure the mental torment and buries his bloody and disheveled head and his face in his hands. He begs for mercy and an end to the torture, but there is no end to his agony.

After a while, the torturing machine drops the soul to the ground level. Then the messengers of hell, who have been watching the soul suffer, surround and mock him, saying, "How could you have been a servant of God? You became an apostle of Satan, and now you are Satan's amusement."

As he listens to the mockery, sobs, and shrieks for mercy, the two fingers on the right hand of the torturing machine pick him up by his neck. Taking no notice of the soul's wriggling, the machine raises him to the height of its neck and pokes his head with its sharp pointed fingernails on its left hand. The machine inflicts additional torment by replaying the slideshow. This torture will continue until the Judgment Day.

Tied Up to the Trunk of a Tree

This is the punishment of a former servant of God, who once taught members of his church and was in charge of many important positions.

Opposing the Holy Spirit

This soul had a strong desire for fame, material gain, and power in his nature. He diligently carried out his duties but did not realize his own wickedness. At one point, he stopped praying, thereby effectively stopped making efforts to circumcise his heart. Unconscientiously, all kinds of evil grew in him like poisonous mushrooms, and when the church he served faced a major crisis, he was immediately taken over by the power of Satan.

When he opposed the Holy Spirit after having been tempted by Satan, his sins became all the more serious because he had been a leader of his church and he influenced so many church members negatively and hindered the kingdom of God.

Subject to both torture and mockery

This man receives a punishment of being tied to the trunk of a tree in the Lower Grave. His punishment is not as severe as that of Judas Iscariot, but it is still harsh and unbearable.

The messenger of hell shows the soul a slideshow that features scenes portraying the happiest moments of his life, mostly of times when he was a faithful servant of God. This mental torment reminds him that he once had a happy time and a chance to receive God's abundant blessings but he never circumcised his heart because of his greed and falsehood, and he is here now to receive this awful punishment.

Hanging from the ceiling are countless black fruit, and after showing the soul a scene from the slideshow, the messenger of hell points to the ceiling and mocks him, saying, "Your greed bore fruit like this!" Then the fruit drops one by one. Each fruit is a head of all those who followed him in confronting God. They committed the same sin with this soul, and the rest of their bodies, after gruesome torture, have been cut off. Only their heads, which are hanging from the ceiling, remain. The soul tied to the tree urged and tempted these people in this world to follow the ways of his greed and do evil, and thus they became the fruit of his greed.

Whenever a servant of Hell mocks him, this mockery serves as a signal to have these fruit drop and burst one by one. Then a head rolls out of the sack with a snap. Dramas, historical or action documentaries, plays, or films in which a character's throat has been slit commonly portray the dead character's head with disheveled hair, a bloody face, blistered lips, and glaring eyes. Heads that fall from the ceiling look quite similar to the heads in such dramas or movies.

Heads fallen from the ceiling gnaw on the soul

When the ghastly heads fall from the ceiling, they cling to the soul one by one. They first cling to his legs and bite them off.

131

Another scene from the slideshow passes before the soul's eyes and the messenger of hell mocks him again, saying, "Look, your greed is hanging like this!" Then, another sack from the ceiling falls, bursts, and another head clings to and virulently bites the soul's arms.

In this manner, whenever the messenger of hell mocks the soul, head from the ceiling falls, one by one. These heads dangle all over the soul's body like a tree bearing abundant fruit. The pain of being bitten by these heads is completely different from that of being bitten by someone or animals in this world. The poison from the sharp teeth of these heads spreads from the bitten parts to the inner bones, and turns the body solid and dark. This pain is so great that being gnawed on by insects or being ripped apart by beasts seems much less painful.

The souls with only their heads left had to suffer the torment of having the rest of their bodies cut off and torn apart. How much grudge would they have against this soul? Even though they confronted God out of their own evil, their desire to pay him back for their fall is that malicious and desperate.

The soul knows very well that he is punished because of his greed. However, instead of regretting or repenting of his sins, he is busy cursing the heads of other souls biting and crushing his body. As time passes and pain increases, the soul becomes all the more wicked and evil.

You must not commit unforgivable sins

I have given five examples of punishments inflicted upon people who confronted God. Such souls are to receive heavier punishments than many others because they, at point in their lives, worked for God to expand His kingdom as leaders in the church.

We must remember here that many of the souls, who have fallen into the Lower Grave and are receiving punishments, all thought they believed God, and faithfully and eagerly served Him, His servants, and His church.

Furthermore, you must remember never to speak against, oppose, or blaspheme the Holy Spirit. The spirit of repentance will not be given to those who oppose the Holy Spirit, especially because they confront the Holy Spirit after they have professed their faith in God and after they have personally experienced the works of the Holy Spirit. Thus, they cannot even repent.

From the early days of my ministry to this day, I have never criticized any other churches or any other servants of God, and never condemned them as "heretics." If other churches and pastors believe in the Triune God, recognize the existence of Heaven and Hell, and preach the message of salvation through Jesus Christ, how can they possibly be heretics?

Moreover, it is clearly confronting the Holy Spirit to condemn and label a church in which or a servant through whom God's authority and presence are displayed and reaffirmed. For such a sin, keep in mind that there is no forgiveness.

Thus, until the truth is ascertained, no one can condemn anyone else as "heretical." In addition, you must never commit the sin of obstructing and confronting the Holy Spirit with your tongue.

If you abandon the God-given duty

We must never abandon God-given duties at our own discretion under any circumstances. Jesus stressed the importance of duty through the parable of the talents (Matthew 25).

There was a man who was going on a journey. He summoned his servants and entrusted his property to them according to each of their ability. He gave five talents to the first servant, two to the second, and one to the last. The first and second servant put their money to work and each gained double. However, the servant who had received one talent went off, dug a hole in the ground, and hid his master's money. After a long time, the master returned and settled accounts with each of them. The men who had received five and two talents respectively presented their other double. The master praised each of them, saying, "Well done, good and faithful servant!" Then the man who had received one talent was forsaken because he did not work with the money and gain any interest on it, but instead just held on to it.

"The talent" in this parable refers to any God-given duty. You see that God forsakes the one who only holds on to his duty. Yet, so many people around us abandon their duties given to them by God. You must realize that those who abandon their duties at their disposal will surely be judged on the Judgment Day.

Cast off hypocrisy and circumcise your heart

Jesus also referred to the importance of the circumcision of your heart when he rebuked the teachers of the law and the Pharisees as hypocrites. The teachers of the law and the Pharisees seemed to live a faithful life, but their hearts were full of evil so Jesus rebuked them, saying that they were like whitewashed tombs.

134

Woe to you, scribes and Pharisees, hypocrites! For you are like whitewashed tombs which on the outside appear beautiful, but inside they are full of dead men's bones and all uncleanness. So you, too, outwardly appear righteous to men, but inwardly you are full of hypocrisy and lawlessness (Matthew 23:27-28).

For the same reason, it is worthless for you to put on your make-up or the fanciest clothes if your heart is full of jealousy, hatred, and arrogance. More than anything else, God wants us to circumcise our hearts and cast off evil.

Evangelizing, caring for church members, and serving the church are all important. However, the most important thing is to love God, walk in the light, and become more and more like God. You should be holy as God is holy and you should be perfect as God is perfect.

On the one hand, if your present zeal for God is not from your true heart and whole faith, it can always degenerate and thus cannot be pleasing to God. On the other hand, if one circumcises his/her heart in order to become holy and whole, the individual's heart will emanate an aroma truly pleasing to God.

Furthermore, no matter how much of God's Word you may have learned and know, the more important thing for you is to set your mind to behave and live in accordance with the Word. You should always keep in mind the existence of the agonizing Hell, purify your heart, and when the Lord Jesus returns, you will be one of the first to embrace Him.

1 Corinthians 2:12-14 tells us, *"Now we have received, not the spirit of the world, but the Spirit who is from God, so that we may know the things freely given to us by God, which things we*

also speak, not in words taught by human wisdom, but in those taught by the Spirit, combining spiritual thoughts with spiritual words. But a natural man does not accept the things of the Spirit of God, for they are foolishness to him; and he cannot understand them, because they are spiritually appraised."

Without the works and help of the Holy Spirit revealed to us by God, how can anyone in the world of flesh speak on spiritual matters and understand them?

God Himself has revealed this testimony of Hell and thus, every part of it is true. Punishments in Hell are so horrific that instead of exposing every detail, I have written of only a few cases of torment. Also, keep in mind that among many people who have fallen into the Lower Grave are those who had once been faithful and loyal to God.

If you do not have proper qualifications, namely, if you stop praying and circumcising your heart, you will almost certainly be tempted by Satan to oppose God and in the end thrown into Hell.

I pray in the name of the Lord that you will grasp how frightening and miserable a place Hell is, strive to save as many souls as you are able, pray fervently, preach the gospel diligently, and always examine yourself in order to reach whole salvation.

Chapter 7

Salvation during the Great Tribulation

When we pay close attention to today's flow of history or the prophecies in the Bible, we realize that the time is ripe and close to the coming of the Lord. In recent years, there have been numerous earthquakes and floods whose magnitudes are matched only about once every hundreds of years.

In addition, frequent large-scale forest fires, hurricanes, and typhoons left behind the paths of destruction and an enormous amount of casualties. In Africa and Asia, many people suffered and died from hunger caused by long droughts. Much of the world has witnessed and experienced abnormal weather caused by the depletion of the ozone layer, "El Niño," "La Niña," and many others.

Moreover, there appears to be no end to wars and conflicts among countries, terrorist acts, and other forms of violence. Atrocities beyond moral principles of man have become an everyday event and been portrayed through mass media.

Such phenomena were already prophesied by Jesus Christ two millennia ago, when He responded to His disciples' question, *"Tell us, when will these things happen, and what will be the sign of Your coming, and of the end of the age?"* (Matthew 24:3)

For instance, how true are the following verses today?

For nation will rise against nation, and kingdom against kingdom, and in various places there will be famines and earthquakes. But all these things are merely the beginning of birth pangs (Matthew 24:7-8).

Therefore, if you have true faith, you should know that the day of Jesus' return is very near and keep watch like the five wise virgins (Matthew 25:1-13). You should never be forsaken like the other five virgins who did not prepare enough oil for their lamps.

Christ's Advent and the Rapture

About two thousand years ago, our Lord Jesus died on the cross, rose again on the third day from the dead, and ascended into Heaven before many people. Acts 1:11 tells us that *"This Jesus, who has been taken up from you into heaven, will come in just the same way as you have watched Him go into heaven."*

Jesus will return in clouds

Jesus Christ has opened the way of salvation, gone into Heaven, been sitting on the right hand of God, and is preparing places for us. At the time of God's choosing and when our places in Heaven are prepared, Jesus will come back to take us as Jesus prophesied in John 14:3, *"If I go and prepare a place for you, I will come again and receive you to Myself, that where I am, there you may be also."*

138

What will the sight to Jesus' return look like?

1 Thessalonians 4:16-17 depicts a scene in which Jesus will come down from Heaven with countless heavenly host and angels, along with the dead in Christ.

For the Lord Himself will descend from Heaven with a shout, with the voice of the archangel and with the trumpet of God, and the dead in Christ will rise first. Then we who are alive and remain will be caught up together with them in the clouds to meet the Lord in the air, and so we shall always be with the Lord.

How magnificent it will be for Jesus Christ to return surrounded and guarded by numerous heavenly host and angels in clouds! At that time, all the people who are saved by faith will be caught up in the air and attend the Seven-year Wedding Banquet.

Those who are already dead but saved in Christ will first resurrect and be caught up in the air, followed by those who are still alive at the time of Jesus' return, whose bodies will transform into imperishable body.

The Rapture and the Seven-year Wedding Banquet

"The Rapture" is an event in which believers will be raised into the air. Where, then, is "the air" mentioned in 1 Thessalonians 4?

According to Ephesians 2:2, saying that *"in which you formerly walked according to the course of this world, according to the prince of the power of the air, of the spirit that is now working in the sons of disobedience,"* "the air" here refers to the place where the evil spirits have authority.

But this place for the evil spirits does not indicate the place of the Seven-year Wedding Banquet. God our Father prepared for the special place for the Banquet. The reason the Bible calls the prepared place the "air" that is the same name for the place for the evil spirits because the two places are in the same space.

When you hazily look up at the sky, you may find it difficult to understand where "the air" – in which we will meet Jesus and where the Seven-year Wedding Banquet will be held – actually is. Answers to such questions are found in "Lectures on Genesis" series and the two-part *Heaven* series. Please refer to those messages because it is vital to correctly understand the spiritual world and believe in the Bible as it is.

Can you imagine how happy will all believers of Jesus, who have been preparing themselves as His bride, be when they finally meet their groom and attend their wedding banquet that is to last for seven years?

> *"Let us rejoice and be glad and give the glory to Him, for the marriage of the Lamb has come and His bride has made herself ready." It was given to her to clothe herself in fine linen, bright and clean; for the fine linen is the righteous acts of the saints. Then he said to me, "Write, 'Blessed are those who are invited to the marriage supper of the Lamb.'" And he said to me, "These are true words of God" (Revelation 19:7-9).*

On the one hand, those believers who have been raised into the air will receive a reward for having overcome the world. On the other hand, those who have not been lifted up will suffer from afflictions of an unimaginable magnitude by the evil spirits who had been driven out from the air to the earth when Jesus returns.

The Seven-year Great Tribulation

While believers who have been saved will enjoy the wedding feast in the air with Jesus Christ for seven years, share joy with Him, and plan their happy future, all those left behind on the earth face tribulations of an unprecedented degree for seven years, and indescribable and frightening disasters will strike the mankind.

World War III and the mark of the beast

During a nuclear war on a global scale to come, World War III, one-third of all trees on the earth will be burnt out and one-third of the humanity will perish. During the same war, it will be difficult to find breathable air and clean water because of severe pollution, and the prices of foodstuffs and necessities will skyrocket.

The mark of the beast, "666," will be presented and everyone will be subject to receive it either on his/her right hand or on forehead. If an individual refuses to receive the mark, his/her identity will not be guaranteed, and he/she will not be able to make any kind of transactions and purchase even the necessities.

And he causes all, the small and the great, and the rich and the poor, and the free men and the slaves, to be given

a mark on their right hand or on their forehead, and he
provides that no one will be able to buy or to sell, except
the one who has the mark, either the name of the beast or
the number of his name. Here is wisdom. Let him who has
understanding calculate the number of the beast, for the
number is that of a man; and his number is six hundred
and sixty-six (Revelation 13:16-18).

Among those left behind after the Lord's Advent and the
Rapture are people who heard the gospel or attended church,
and now remember the Word of God.

There are those who deliberately abandoned their faith, and
others who thought they believed God but are still left behind.
If these had believed the Bible wholeheartedly, they would have
led good lives in Christ.

Instead, they were always lukewarm and told themselves,
"I will find out whether or not Heaven and Hell exist only
after I die," and thus did not have the kind of faith required for
salvation.

Punishments for people receiving the mark of the beast

Such people realize that every Word in the Bible is true only
after they witness the Rapture. They grieve and weep bitterly.
Seized by great fear, they repent of not having lived according
to the will of God and desperately seek a way to salvation.
Furthermore, because they know that receiving the mark of the
beast will only lead them to Hell, they do all they can to avoid
receiving it. Even in this way, they will try to prove their faith.

Then another angel, a third one, followed them, saying

with a loud voice, "If anyone worships the beast and his image, and receives a mark on his forehead or on his hand, he also will drink of the wine of the wrath of God, which is mixed in full strength in the cup of His anger; and he will be tormented with fire and brimstone in the presence of the holy angels and in the presence of the Lamb. And the smoke of their torment goes up forever and ever; they have no rest day and night, those who worship the beast and his image, and whoever receives the mark of his name." Here is the perseverance of the saints who keep the commandments of God and their faith in Jesus (Revelation 14:9-12).

However, it is not easy to refuse the mark of the beast especially in a world in which the evil spirits have completely taken over everything. At the same time, the evil spirits also know that these people will receive salvation when they refuse the 666 mark and die martyr's death. Thus, the evil spirits will not and cannot easily give up.

During the days of the early Christian church two thousand years ago, many government authorities persecuted Christians by crucifying, beheading, or abandoning them as lion's prey. If one were persecuted and killed in this way, countless people would receive a quick death during the Seven-year Great Tribulation. However, the evil spirits during this seven-year span will not make things any easy for the people left behind. The evil spirits will force people to deny Jesus in any way they can by mobilizing every resource they have against the people. This does not mean that people can commit suicide to avoid the torment, because suicide only leads to Hell.

Those who will become martyrs

I already mentioned some of the cruel torture methods used by the evil spirits. During the Great Tribulation, torturing methods beyond imagination will be freely used. Moreover, because the torment is almost impossible to endure, only a small number of people actually receive salvation during this period.

Therefore, all of us must be spiritually awake at all times and possess the kind of faith that will lift us into the air at the time of Christ's Advent.

While I was praying, God showed me a vision in which people left behind after the Rapture were receiving all kinds of tortures. I saw that most people were not able to endure them and succumbed to the evil spirits in the end.

The torture ranges from peeling off people's skin, to breaking and shattering their joints, to chopping off their fingers and toes and pouring sizzling oil over them. Some people who are able to withstand their own torment cannot stand seeing their elderly parents or little children suffer and they, too, succumb to the 666 mark.

Still, there are a small number of righteous people who overcome all the temptations and torment. These people receive salvation. Even though it is shameful salvation and they enter Paradise belonging to Heaven, they are just grateful and glad that they do not fall into Hell.

This is why we are obligated to spread this message of Hell all over the world. Even if it appears as though people are not paying attention now, if they remember it during the Great Tribulation, it will pave the way of their salvation.

Some people say that they will die martyr's death to receive salvation if the Rapture really occurs and they are left behind.

However, if they could not have faith in this time of peace, how would they possibly defend their faith in the midst of such brutal torment? We cannot even foretell what will happen to us in the next ten minutes. If they die before even receiving an opportunity to die a martyr's death, only Hell awaits them.

Martyrdom During the Great Tribulation

To help you understand the torment of the Great Tribulation more easily and allow you to stay spiritually awake so that you may avoid it, let me explain further with the example of a soul.

Since this woman received God's overflowing grace, she could see and hear great, glorious, and even hidden things about God. Yet, her heart was filled with evil, and she had little faith.

With such gifts from God, she carried out important duties, played a crucial role in expanding the kingdom of God, and often pleased God with her deeds. It is easy for people to presume, "Those people with important duties in the church must be men and women of great faith!"

Yet, this is not necessarily true. From God's perspective, there are countless believers whose faiths are actually anything but "great." God measures not fleshly faith, but spiritual faith.

God wants spiritual faith

Let us briefly examine the "spiritual faith" through the case of the deliverance of the Israelites out of Egypt. The Israelites witnessed and experienced God's Ten Plagues. They witnessed the Red Sea split in half and Pharaoh and his army drown in it. They experienced God's guidance through the pillar of cloud by day and the pillar of fire by night. Everyday they ate manna from Heaven, heard the voice of God seated in the clouds, and saw His workings with fire. They drank the water from a rock after Moses had struck it, and saw bitter water at Marah turn sweet. Even though they witnessed repeatedly the works and signs of the living God, their faith was neither pleasing nor acceptable to God. Thus, they could not enter the Promised Land of Canaan in the end (Numbers 20:12).

On the one hand, one's faith without action, no matter how much one knows God's Word and has witnessed and heard His works and miracles, is not true faith. On the other hand, if we come to possess spiritual faith, we will not stop learning God's Word; we will become obedient to the Word, circumcise our hearts, and avoid every kind of evil. Whether we have "great" or "little" faith is determined by the extent to which we are obedient to God's Word, behave and live according to it, and resemble the heart of God.

Repeated disobedience in arrogance

In this aspect, the woman had little faith. She tried to circumcise her heart for a while but could not completely abandon evil. In addition, because she was in the position of preaching the Word of God, she became all the more arrogant.

The woman thought she had true and great faith. She went as far as to think God's will could not be fulfilled or carried out without her presence or assistance. Increasingly, instead of giving glory to God for her God-given gifts, she wanted to take the credit herself. Furthermore, she used God's possession at her disposal in order to satisfy the desires of her sinful nature.

She continued to disobey repeatedly. Even if she knew it was God's will for her to head east, she headed west. The way God abandoned Saul the first king of Israel because of his disobedience (1 Samuel 15:22-23), even if people were once used as God's tools to fulfill and expand God's kingdom, repeated disobedience will only instigate God to turn His face away from them.

Because the woman knew the Word, she was aware of her sins and repeatedly repented. However, her prayer of repentance was only with her lips, not from her heart. She ended up committing the same sins repeatedly, thereby further heightening the wall of sin between God and herself.

2 Peter 2:22 tells us, *"It has happened to them according to the true proverb, 'A dog returns to its own vomit,' and, 'A sow, after washing, returns to wallowing in the mire.'"* After repenting of her sins, she committed the same sins time after time.

In the end, because she was seized in her own arrogance, greed, and countless sins, God turned His face from her and she eventually became a device of Satan in opposing God.

When the final opportunity to repent is given

Generally, those who speak against, oppose, or blaspheme the Holy Spirit cannot be forgiven. Never again will they receive an opportunity to repent, and they will end up in the Lower Grave.

Yet, there is something different about this woman. Despite all the sins and evil that upset God over and over again, He has still left one last opportunity for her to repent. This is because the woman once was God's invaluable device for His kingdom. Even if the woman abandoned her duty and the promise of the glory and rewards of Heaven, because she had greatly pleased God, He is giving her one, last chance.

She still opposes God, and the Holy Spirit within her has become extinct. However, through God's special grace, the woman has one final opportunity to repent and receive salvation during the Great Tribulation through martyrdom.

Her thoughts are still trapped under Satan's control but after the Rapture, she will come to her senses. Because she knows the Word of God so well, she is also well aware of the path ahead. After realizing that the only way to receive salvation is martyrdom, she will thoroughly repent, gather around Christians left behind, worship, praise, and pray with them as she prepares for her martyrdom.

Martyr's death and shameful salvation

When the time comes, she will refuse to receive the 666 mark and be subsequently taken away to be tortured by those controlled by Satan. They peel off her skin layer by layer. They even sear the softest and most private parts of her body with fire. They will devise a method for her torment to be the most painful and to last the longest. Soon the room is filled with the smell of burning flesh. Her body is smeared in blood from head to toe, her head is facing down, and her face is tinged dark and blue, resembling a corpse.

If she can endure this torment to the end, despite her countless sins and evil of the past, she will receive at least the shameful salvation and enter Paradise. In Paradise, the outskirts of Heaven and the farthest place from the Throne of God, the woman will lament and tear for her deeds in this life. Of course, she will be grateful and joyous for having been saved. Yet, for ages to come she will regret and long for New Jerusalem, saying, "Only if I had abandoned evil and carried out God's duty wholeheartedly, I would be in the most glorious place within New Jerusalem..." When she sees people she knew in this life living in New Jerusalem, she will always feel ashamed and embarrassed.

If she receives the 666 mark

If she does not endure the torment and receive the mark of the beast, before the Millennium, she will be thrown into the Lower Grave and punished by being crucified on a cross on the right rear of Judas Iscariot. Her punishments in the Lower Grave are the repetition of the torture she received during the Great Tribulation. Over a thousand years, the skin of her body will be peeled off and seared with fire repeatedly.

The messengers of hell and all those who did evil by following her will torture the woman. They are also punished according to their evil deeds and vent out their pain and anger on her.

They are punished in this way in the Lower Grave until the end of the Millennium. After the Judgment, those souls will go to Hell burning with fire and sulfur, where only severer punishments await them.

Christ's Second Advent and the Millennium

As mentioned above, Jesus Christ returns in the air and those who are taken up will enjoy seven years of a wedding banquet with Him, while the Great Tribulation gets under way by the evil spirits who have been driven out from the air.

Then, Jesus Christ returns to the earth and the Millennium begins. The evil spirits are confined in the Abyss during this time. Those who attended the Seven-year Wedding Banquet and those who died martyr's death during the Great Tribulation rule over the earth and share love with Jesus Christ for a thousand years.

> *Blessed and holy is the one who has a part in the first resurrection; over these the second death has no power, but they will be priests of God and of Christ and will reign with Him for a thousand years (Revelation 20: 6).*

A small number of fleshly people who survived the Great Tribulation will also live on the earth during the Millennium. However, those who already died without receiving salvation will continue to be punished in the Lower Grave.

The Millennium Kingdom

When the Millennium comes, people will enjoy a peaceful life like the days of the Garden of Eden, because there is no evil spirit. Jesus Christ and the saved, spiritual people live in a city resembling castles of kings separated from the people of flesh. Spiritual people live in the city and people of flesh who survived the Great Tribulation live outside this city.

Before the Millennium, Jesus Christ cleanses the earth. He purifies the polluted air, and renews trees, plants, mountains, and streams. He creates a beautiful environment.

The people of flesh strive to give birth as often and many times as they can because there are only a few of them left. Clean air and the absence of evil spirit leave no room for disease and evil. Unrighteousness and evil in the heart of the people of flesh are not revealed during this time because in the Abyss are confined the evil spirits who emanate evil.

Like the days prior to Noah's, people will live for hundreds of years. The earth is soon filled with countless people for a thousand years. People do not eat meat but fruit because there is no destruction of life at all.

Furthermore, it will take a great deal of time for them to reach the level of today's scientific advancement because much of the civilization will have been destroyed in wars during the Great Tribulation. As time passes, the level of their civilization may reach that of today as they increase their wisdom and knowledge.

Spiritual people and fleshly people dwell together

It is not necessary for spiritual people living with Jesus Christ on the earth to eat the way people of flesh do, because the bodies of the former group have already been transformed into resurrected, spiritual bodies. They usually consume the aroma of flowers and the like, but if they wish, they may have the same food as the people of flesh. However, spiritual people do not enjoy physical food and even if they eat it, they do not excrete wastes the way people of flesh do. As the resurrected Jesus breathed after He had a piece of fish, the food that

151

spiritual people consume is decomposed into the air through breathing.

The spiritual people also preach and testify Jesus Christ to the people of flesh, so that at the end of the Millennium when the evil spirits are briefly released from the Abyss, the people of flesh will not be tempted. The time is before the Judgment, so God has not confined the evil spirits permanently in the Abyss but only for a thousand years (Revelation 20:3).

At the end of the Millennium

When the Millennium ends, the evil spirits who have been confined in the Abyss for the thousand years are briefly released. They begin to tempt and delude the people of flesh who have been living peacefully. Most people of flesh are tempted and deluded no matter how much spiritual people have taught them against it. Even though the spiritual people have warned in detail about the things to come, people of flesh are nevertheless tempted and plan to confront and wage war against the spiritual people.

> *When the thousand years are completed, Satan will be released from his prison, and will come out to deceive the nations which are in the four corners of the earth, Gog and Magog, to gather them together for the war; the number of them is like the sand of the seashore. And they came up on the broad plain of the earth and surrounded the camp of the saints and the beloved city, and fire came down from Heaven and devoured them (Revelation 20:7-9).*

However, God will destroy by fire the people of flesh who waged war, and will throw the evil spirits that have been briefly released back into the Abyss after the Judgment of the Great White Throne.

In the end, the people of flesh who increase in number during the Millennium will also be judged according to God's justice. On the one hand, all the people who did not receive salvation – among whom are those who have survived the Seven Years of Great Tribulation – are cast into Hell. On the other hand, those who have received salvation will enter Heaven and, according to their faith, will reside in different places within Heaven, i.e. New Jerusalem, Paradise, et cetera.

After the Judgment of the Great White Throne, the spiritual world is divided into Heaven and Hell. On this, I will explain further in the following chapter.

Preparing to Be the Lord's Beautiful Bride

To avoid being left behind in the Great Tribulation, you have to prepare yourself as a beautiful bride of Jesus Christ and greet Him at His Advent.

Matthew 25:1-13 is the parable of the ten virgins, which serves as a great lesson for all believers. Even if you may confess your faith in God, you will not be able to greet your bridegroom Jesus Christ if you do not have enough oil prepared for your lamp. Five virgins prepared their oil so they could greet their bridegroom and enter the wedding banquet. The other five virgins did not prepare oil and could not join the banquet.

How, then, can we prepare ourselves like the five wise

virgins, become a bride of the Lord, and avoid falling into the Great Tribulation but instead partake in the Wedding Banquet?

Pray fervently and keep alert

Even if you are a new believer and have weak faith, so long as you do your best to circumcise your heart, God will keep you safe even in the midst of fiery trials. No matter how difficult the circumstances are, God will wrap you with a blanket of life and make you overcome any trials with ease.

However, God cannot protect even those who may have been believers for a long time, have carried out God-given duties, and know a great deal of the Word of God, if they stop their prayer, stop admiring purification, and stop circumcising their hearts.

When you face difficulties, you must be able to discern the voice of the Holy Spirit to overcome them. Yet, if you do not pray, how would you listen to the voice of the Holy Spirit and lead a victorious life? As you are not filled completely with the Holy Spirit, you increasingly rely on your own thoughts and stumble time after time, tempted by Satan.

Furthermore, now that we are approaching the end of the age, the evil spirits prowl around like roaring lions in search of someone to devour because they know their end is also near. We often see a lazy student cramming and losing his/her sleep in days leading up to exams. Similarly, if you are a believer who is aware that we are living in days leading up to the end of the age, you must keep alert and prepare yourself as a beautiful bride of the Lord.

Abandon evil and resemble the Lord

What kinds of people keep themselves alert? They always pray, are always full of the Holy Spirit, believe in the Word of God, and live according to His Word.

When you keep alert all the time, you will always be communicating with God so you cannot be temped by evil spirits. In addition, you can easily overcome any trials because the Holy Spirit makes you aware of things to come in advance, leads your path, and allows you to realize the Word of truth.

Yet, those who do not keep alert cannot hear the voice of the Holy Spirit so they are easily tempted by Satan, and go to the way of death. Keeping alert is to circumcise your heart, behave and live according to the Word of God, and become sanctified.

Revelation 22:14 tells us that *"Blessed are those who wash their robes, so that they may have the right to the tree of life, and may enter by the gates into the city."* In this passage, "robes" refer to formal attire. Spiritually, "robes" refer to your heart and your conduct. To "wash your robes" symbolizes casting off evil and following God's Word to become spiritual and become more and more like Jesus Christ. Those who are sanctified this way earn the right to enter the gates of Heaven and enjoy eternal life.

People who wash their robes in faith

How can we thoroughly wash our robes? You must first circumcise your heart with the Word of truth and fervent prayer. In other words, you must throw away any untruth and evil from your heart and fill it only with truth. Just as you wash away filth on your clothing in clean water, you should wash away dirty sins, lawlessness, and evil in your heart with the Word of God, the water of life, and put on the robes of the truth and resemble the heart of Jesus Christ. God will bless anyone who has displayed faith in deed and circumcised his/her heart.

Revelation 3:5 tells us, *"He who overcomes will thus be clothed in white garments; and I will not erase his name from the book of life, and I will confess his name before My Father and before His angels."* People who overcome the world in faith and walk in the truth will enjoy eternal life in Heaven because they possess the heart of the truth and no evil can be found in them.

Instead, people who dwell in the darkness have nothing to do with God no matter how long they may have been Christians, because they will surely have a name that they are alive, but they are dead (Revelation 3:1). Therefore, always put your hope only in God who does not judge us by our appearance but only examines our hearts and deeds. Also, always pray and obey the Word of God so that you may reach perfect salvation.

Chapter 8

Punishments in Hell
after the Great Judgment

With Christ's Advent the Millennium begins on this earth and after that the Judgment of the Great White Throne follows. The Judgment – which will determine Heaven or Hell, and rewards or punishments – will judge everyone according to what he/she has done in this life. Thus, some will enjoy eternal happiness in Heaven and others be punished forever in Hell. Let us delve into the Judgment of the Great White Throne, through which Heaven or Hell is decided, and what kind of place Hell is.

Unsaved Souls Fall into Hell
after the Judgment

In July 1982, while I was praying in preparation for the beginning of my ministry, I came to know about the Judgment of the Great White Throne in detail. God showed me a scene in which He was seated in His Throne, the Lord Jesus Christ and Moses standing in front of the Throne, and those who were playing the role of jury. Even though God judges with accuracy and fairness not comparable to those of any judges in the world, He will make rulings with Jesus Christ as an attorney with love, Moses as a prosecutor of the Law, and the people as jurors.

Punishments of Hell are decided at the Judgment

Revelation 20:11-15 tells us how God judges with accuracy and justice. The Judgment is carried out with the Book of Life in which the names of the saved are recorded and the books in which every deed of people is recorded.

Then I saw a great white throne and Him who sat upon it, from whose presence earth and Heaven fled away, and no place was found for them. And I saw the dead, the great and the small, standing before the throne, and books were opened; and another book was opened, which is the book of life; and the dead were judged from the things which were written in the books, according to their deeds. And the sea gave up the dead which were in it, and death and Hades gave up the dead which were in them; and they were judged, every one of them according to their deeds. Then death and Hades were thrown into the lake of fire. This is the second death, the lake of fire. And if anyone's name was not found written in the book of life, he was thrown into the lake of fire.

"The dead" here refers to all those who have not accepted Christ as their Savior or have dead faith. When the time of God's choosing arrives, "the dead" resurrect and stand before the Throne of God to be judged. The Book of Life is opened in front of the Throne of God.

Besides the Book of Life, in which the names of all saved people are recorded, there are other books in which every deed of the dead is recorded. The angels record everything we do, say, and think, i.e. cursing others, striking someone, flying into a rage, doing good, and so on. Just as you can keep vivid records of certain events and dialogues for a long time with a video camera or recorders of various types, God the Almighty also maintains every scene of one's life on the earth.

Thus, God will judge in justice on the Judgment Day according to the records in these books. Those who have not been saved will be judged according to their evil deeds, and will receive various types of punishments according to the severity of their sins, eternally in Hell.

The lake of fire or of burning sulfur

The part "the sea gave up the dead which were in it" does not mean that the sea gave up those who had drowned in it. "The sea" here spiritually refers to the world. It means that those who lived in the world and returned to dust will resurrect in order to be judged before God.

What, then, does it mean to say, "Death and Hades gave up the dead which were in them"? It means that those who have suffered in Hades, referred to as the Lower Grave, will also resurrect and stand before God to be judged. After being judged by God, most of those who have suffered in the Lower Grave will be thrown into the lake of fire or burning sulfur according to the severity of their sins because, as mentioned above, the punishments of the Lower Grave are given until the Judgment of the Great White Throne occurs.

But for the cowardly and unbelieving and abominable and murderers and immoral persons and sorcerers and idolaters and all liars, their part will be in the lake that burns with fire and brimstone, which is the second death (Revelation 21:8).

Punishments in the lake of fire cannot possibly be compared to those in the Lower Grave. It is described in Mark 9:47-49, *"If your eye causes you to stumble, throw it out; it is better for you to enter the kingdom of God with one eye, than, having two eyes, to be cast into Hell, where their worm does not die, and the fire is not quenched. For everyone will be salted with fire."* Moreover, the lake of burning sulfur is seven times hotter than the lake of fire.

Until the Judgment, people are torn by insects and beasts, tortured by the messengers of hell, or suffer from various kinds of punishments in the Lower Grave which serves as a waiting place en route to Hell. After the Judgment, only the pain from the lake of fire and burning sulfur will remain.

Agony in the lake of fire or of burning sulfur

When I delivered the messages on these ghastly sights of the Lower Grave, many of my church members found themselves unable to hold back tears or shudder with lament for those in such a wretched place. However, sufferings from punishments in the lake of fire or burning sulfur are much severer than any punishment in the Lower Grave. Can you imagine the magnitude of torment even a little? Even if we try, there is a limit for us, who are still in flesh, to understand spiritual concepts.

Similarly, how can we possibly understand the glory and beauty of Heaven to the fullest extent? The word "eternity" itself is not something with which we are familiar and we are forced to merely conjecture. Even if we try to imagine life in Heaven based on "joy," "happiness," "enchantment," "beauty," and the like, it is not comparable to the actual life we will some day live in Heaven. When you actually go to Heaven, see everything with your own eyes, and experience life, your jaw will drop to the ground and you will be speechless. Likewise, unless we actually experience the torment of Hell, we can never fully grasp the magnitude and amount of suffering that is beyond the limits of this world.

Those who fall into the lake of fire or burning sulfur

Even though I will try my best, please keep in mind that Hell is not a place that can be adequately described with the words of this world, and even if I do explain to the best of my ability, my description will account for less than one-millionth of the gruesome reality of Hell. Furthermore, when they remember that the length of torment is not limited but will last forever more, the condemned souls are forced to suffer even more.

After the Judgment of the Great White Throne, those who received the first and the second levels of punishment in the Lower Grave will be thrown into the lake of fire. Those who received the third and fourth levels of punishments will be thrown into the lake of burning sulfur. Souls currently in the Lower Grave know that the Judgment is still to come, and they know where they will be after the Judgment. Even as they are ripped apart by insects and the messengers of hell, these souls can see the lake of fire and burning sulfur in Hell from a distance and are well aware that they will be punished there.

Thus, souls in the Lower Grave suffer from not only their present pain, but also a mental torment in fear of things to come after the Judgment.

A cry of lamentation from a soul in the Lower Grave

While I was praying for revelations on Hell, through the Holy Spirit God allowed me to hear a cry of lamentation from a soul in the Lower Grave. When I write every word of the lamentation, try to feel even a bit of fear and despair engulfing this soul.

How can this be a figure of a human being?
This is not how I looked during my life on Earth.
My appearance here is appalling and revolting!

In this endless pain and despair,
how can I be set free?
What can I do to escape from this?
Can I die? What can I do?
Can I get some rest even for a while
in the midst of this eternal punishment?
Is there any way to cut this damned life short
from this unbearable pain?

I hurt my body to kill myself, but I cannot die.
There is no end...there is just no end...
There is no end to the torment of my soul.
There is no end to my enduring life.

How can I describe this with words?
I will soon be thrown
into a wide and depthless lake of fire.
How am I to endure it?

Torment here is unbearable as it is!
That raging lake of fire is
so scary, so deep, and so hot.
How am I to endure it?
How can I escape from it?
How can I possibly escape from this torment?

Only if I could live...
Only if there were a way for me to live...
Only if I could be delivered...
I could at least look for a way out,
but I cannot see it.

There are only darkness, despair, and pain here,
and there are only frustration and hardship for me.
How am I to endure this torment?
Only if He would open the door for life...
Only if I could see a way out of this...

Please save me. Please save me.
It is too frightening and difficult for me to endure.
Please save me. Please save me.
My days so far have been painful and hurtful.
How am I to go into that fiery lake?
Please save me!
Please look at me!

Please save me!
Please have mercy on me!
Please save me!
Please save me!

Once you are cast into the Lower Grave

After the end of life on the earth, no one receives "a second chance." Only the bearing the burden of your every deed awaits you.

When people hear about the existence of Heaven and Hell, some say, "I'll find out after I die." However, once you are dead, it is too late. Because there is no turning back once you die, you have to know this for sure before you die.

Once you are cast into the Lower Grave, no matter how much you regret, repent, and beg God, you cannot avoid the inevitable and horrible punishments. There is no hope for your future but only the endless torment and despair.

The soul who laments as above knows all too well that there is no way or possibility of salvation. Nevertheless, the soul is crying out to God "just in case." The soul is begging for mercy and for salvation. This soul's cry turns into piercing blubber, and this shriek only whirls around the expanse of Hell and disappears. Of course, there is no response.

However, the repentance of people in the Lower Grave is not sincere and earnest even though they seemingly repent so pitifully. Since the wickedness in their hearts still remains and they know their shrieks are useless, these souls emanate more evil and curse God. This evidently shows us why such individuals could not enter Heaven in the first place.

The Lake of Fire
& the Lake of Burning Sulfur

In the Lower Grave, the souls can at least implore, reproach, and lament, asking themselves, "Why am I here?" They also fear the lake of fire and think of ways to escape the torment, thinking, 'Now, how can I escape from that messenger of hell?'

Once thrown into the lake of fire, however, they cannot think about anything else because of the agonizing and endless pain. Punishments in the Lower Grave were relatively light, compared to those in the lake of fire. Punishments in the lake of fire are unimaginably painful. It is so painful that we cannot understand or envision it with our limited capacities.

Put salt on a hot frying pan if you want to imagine even a little bit of the torment. You will see the salt popping, and this resembles the scene in the lake of fire: the souls are like the popping salt.

Also, imagine that you are in a pool of boiling water, measured at 100°C. The lake of fire is much hotter than the boiling water, and the lake of burning sulfur is seven times hotter than the lake of fire. Once you are thrown in it, there is no way to escape and you will suffer forever and ever. The first, second, third, and fourth levels of punishments in the Lower Grave before the Judgment are much easier to endure.

Why does God, then, let them suffer in the Lower Grave for a thousand years before tossing them into the lake of fire or the lake of burning sulfur? The unsaved people will reflect themselves. God wants them to figure out for what reasons they were destined to such a wretched place as Hell, and thoroughly repent for the sins of the past. However, it is extremely difficult to find people who repent, and rather they emanate more evil than ever before. Now we know why God must have made Hell.

Being salted with fire in the lake of fire

While I was praying in 1982, God showed me a scene from the Judgment of the Great White Throne, and briefly the lake of fire and the lake of burning sulfur. These two lakes were very vast.

From a distance, the two lakes and the souls in them looked like people in hot springs. Some people were submerged to the chest, while others were submerged to the neckline, exposing only their heads.

In Mark 9:48-49, Jesus spoke of Hell as a place *"where their worm does not die, and the fire is not quenched. For everyone will be salted with fire."* Can you imagine the pain in such an awful environment? As these souls try to escape, all they can manage to do is to jump like the popping salt and gnash their teeth.

Sometimes people in this world jump up and down as they play or as they dance late into the night at clubs. After a while, they get tired and rest if they want. In Hell, however, the souls jump not out of pleasure but because of extreme pain and, of course, there is no rest with them even if they want. They scream in pain so loudly that they become lightheaded, and their glancing eyes turn deep blue and become ghastly bloodshot. Furthermore, their brains burst and liquids are gushing out.

No matter how desperately they try, the souls cannot get out. They try to push away and trample on one another but it is useless. Every inch of the lake of fire, whose one end is invisible from the other end, maintains the same temperature, and the temperature of the lake does not decrease even with the passing of time. Until the Judgment of the Great White Throne, the Lower Grave has been controlled by the command of Lucifer, and all punishments have been given according to Lucifer's power and authority.

After the Judgment, however, punishments will be given by God and administered according to His providence and power. Thus, the temperature of the entire lake of fire can be always maintained at the same level.

This fire will make the souls suffer but will not kill them. Just as the body parts of the souls in the Lower Grave restore even after they are cut out or ripped apart into pieces, the bodies of the souls in Hell are quickly restored soon after they are scorched.

The whole body and organs therein scorched

How are the souls in the lake of fire punished? Have you ever watched a scene from comic books, animated films, or cartoon series on television in which a character is electrocuted by "high-voltage" electricity? The moment he is electrocuted, his body turns into a skeleton with a dark-colored outline surrounding his body. When he is released from the flow of electricity, he appears normal. Or, picture X-ray scans that show the inner parts of the human body.

In a similar way, the souls in the lake of fire are shown in their physical form in one moment. In the next, the bodies are nowhere to be seen and only their spirits are visible. This pattern repeats itself. In the scorching fire, the bodies of the souls are burnt in an instant and disappear, and then they are soon restored.

In this world, when you suffer a third-degree burn, you may not be able to endure the stifling sensation all over the body and go mad. No one else can understand degree of this pain until he himself experiences it. You may not be able to endure the pain even only if your arms have been burned.

Generally, the stifling sensation does not go away soon after the burn but lasts for a few days. The heat of fire infiltrates the body, and hurts cells, sometimes even the heart. Then, how much more painful will it be to have all your body parts and internal organs scorched, only to have them restored and scorched repeatedly?

Souls in the lake of fire cannot endure the pain but they cannot faint, die, or take a rest even for a moment.

The lake of burning sulfur

The lake of fire is a place of punishments for those who committed relatively lighter sins and suffered from the first or second level of punishments in the Lower Grave. Those who committed heavier sins and suffered from the third and fourth levels of punishments in the Lower Grave will enter the lake of burning sulfur, which is seven times hotter than the lake of fire. As mentioned above, the lake of burning sulfur is reserved for the following people: those who spoke against, opposed, and blasphemed the Holy Spirit; those who crucified Jesus Christ all over again; those who betrayed Him; those who kept on deliberately sinning; extreme idolaters; those who sinned after having their conscience branded; all those who opposed God with evil deeds; and false prophets and teachers who taught lies.

The entire lake of fire is filled with "red" fire. The lake of burning sulfur is filled with more "yellow" than "red" fire and is always boiling with bubbles the size of gourds here and there. The souls in this lake are completely submerged in the boiling liquid of burning sulfur.

Overwhelmed by pain

How can you explain the pain in the lake of burning sulfur that is seven times hotter than the lake of fire in which the pain is also unimaginable?

Let me explain with an analogy of things in this world. If someone were to drink liquid that is melted from iron in a blast furnace, how painful would that be? His internal organs will be burnt when the heat, hot enough to melt hard iron into liquid, enters his stomach down his throat.

In the lake of fire, the souls can at least jump or shout in pain. In the lake of burning sulfur, however, the souls cannot moan or think but are only oppressed by pain. The degree of torment and agony to be endured in the lake of burning sulfur cannot be described with any gestures or words. Moreover, the souls have to suffer eternally. Then, how can this kind of torment be possibly described with words?

Some Remain in the Lower Grave Even After the Judgment

Saved people of Old Testament times had been in the Upper Grave until Jesus Christ resurrected, and after His resurrection, they entered Paradise and will wait in the Waiting Place in Paradise until His Second Advent in the air takes place. On the one hand, saved people of New Testament times adjust themselves in the Upper Grave for three days and enter the Waiting Place in Paradise and wait there until Jesus Christ's Second Coming in the Air.

However, unborn children who die in their mother's wombs do not go to Paradise either after the resurrection of Jesus Christ or even after the Judgment. They dwell in the Upper Grave forever.

Similarly, among those who currently suffer in the Lower Grave are exceptions. These souls are not thrown into either the lake of fire or the lake of burning sulfur even after the Judgment. Who are they?

Children who die before puberty

Among the unsaved are aborted fetuses of the age of six months or later into the pregnancy and children before the puberty years, about the age of twelve. These souls are not cast into the lake of fire or burning sulfur. This is because even though they come to the Lower Grave by their own evil, at the time of their death they are not mature enough to possess an independent will of their own. This means that their life in faith may not necessarily have been the course they select, because they could be easily influenced by external elements such as their parents, ancestors, and environments.

The God of love and justice considers these factors and does not throw them into the lake of fire or the lake of burning sulfur even after the Judgment. This does not mean, however, that their punishments will diminish or disappear. They will be punished eternally the way they were punished in the Lower Grave.

Since the wages of sin is death

Except for that case, all people in the Lower Grave will be cast into the lake of fire or burning sulfur according to their sins committed while they were cultivated on the earth. In Romans 6:23 it is read that, *"For the wages of sin is death, but the free gift of God is eternal life in Christ Jesus our Lord."* Here, "death" does not refer to the end of life on the earth, but means the eternal punishment in either the lake of fire or burning sulfur. The terrible and agonizing torment of the eternal punishment is the wages of sin, and thus, you know sin is terrible, filthy, and vile.

If people knew even a little about the eternal misery of Hell, how could they not be scared to go to Hell? How could they not accept Jesus Christ, obey, and live by the Word of God?

Jesus told us the following in Mark 9:45-47:

If your foot causes you to stumble, cut it off; it is better for you to enter life lame, than, having your two feet, to be cast into Hell, where their worm does not die, and the fire is not quenched. If your eye causes you to stumble, throw it out; it is better for you to enter the kingdom of God with one eye, than, having two eyes, to be cast into Hell.

It is better for you to cut off your feet if you commit sins by going to places you should not be going than to fall into Hell. It is better for you to cut off your hands if you commit sins

171

by doing things that should not be done than to go to Hell. Similarly, it is also better for you to pluck your eye out if you commit sins by seeing things you should not see.

However, with the grace of God freely given to us, we do not have to cut off our hands and feet or pluck our eyes in order to enter Heaven. This is because our sinless and blameless Lamb, Lord Jesus Christ, was crucified on our behalf, had His hands and feet nailed and wore a crown of thorns.

Son of God came to destroy the devil's work

Therefore, whoever believes in the blood of Jesus Christ is forgiven, freed from the punishment of the lake of fire or burning sulfur, and rewarded eternal life.

1 John 3:7-9 tells us, *"Little children, make sure no one deceives you; the one who practices righteousness is righteous, just as He is righteous; the one who practices sin is of the devil; for the devil has sinned from the beginning. The Son of God appeared for this purpose, to destroy the works of the devil. No one who is born of God practices sin, because His seed abides in him; and he cannot sin, because he is born of God."*

Sin is more than deed, such as stealing, murdering, or swindling. Evil in one's heart is a more serious sin. God loathes evil in our hearts. He hates evil heart itself that judges and condemns others, evil heart that hates and stumbles, and evil heart that is cunning and betraying. What will Heaven be like if people with such hearts were allowed to enter and live in it? Even in Heaven, then, people will argue over right and wrong, so God does not allow evil men to enter Heaven.

Therefore, if you become a child of God empowered by the blood of Jesus Christ, you must not follow the untruth anymore or serve as a slave to the devil, but live in the truth as a child of God, who is the light itself. Only then can you possess all the glory of Heaven, gain blessings to enjoy the authority as a child of God and prosper even in this world.

You must not commit sins professing your faith

God loves us so much that He sent His beloved, innocent, and one and only Son to die for us on a cross. Can you imagine, then, how much God will lament and be upset when He sees those claiming to be "God's children" commit sins, under the influence of the devil, and advance towards Hell ever so quickly?

I ask you not to commit sins but obey God's command, proving yourself as God's precious child. When you do that, all your prayers will be answered more swiftly and you will become a true child of God, and in the end, you will enter and live in the glorious New Jerusalem. You will also gain the power and authority to drive away the darkness from those who do not yet know the truth, still commit sins, and are becoming slaves to the devil. You will be empowered to lead them to God.

May you be a true child of God, receive answers to all your prayers and requests, glorify Him, and deliver countless people from the path to Hell, so that you can reach the glory of God, shining like the sun in Heaven.

Evil Spirits to Be Confined in the Abyss

According to *The Webster's New World College Dictionary,* the term "Abyss" is defined as a "bottomless gulf," "chasm," or "anything too deep for measurement." In the biblical sense, the Abyss is the deepest and lowest part in Hell. It is reserved only for the evil spirits that are irrelevant to the human cultivation.

Then I saw an angel coming down from heaven, holding the key of the abyss and a great chain in his hand. And he laid hold of the dragon, the serpent of old, who is the devil and Satan, and bound him for a thousand years; and he threw him into the abyss, and shut it and sealed it over him, so that he would not deceive the nations any longer, until the thousand years were completed; after these things he must be released for a short time (Revelation 20:1-3).

This is a description of a time towards the end of the Seven-year Great Tribulation. After Jesus Christ's Advent, evil spirits will control the world for seven years, during which World War III and other disasters are unleashed all over the world. After the Great Tribulation is the Millennium Kingdom, during which the evil spirits are confined in the Abyss. Towards the end of the Millennium, the evil spirits are set free for a short time and when the Judgment of the Great White Throne is complete, they will be locked again in the Abyss and this time, for good. Lucifer and his servants control the world of darkness, but after the Judgment, Heaven and Hell will be administered only by God's power.

Evil spirits are only instruments for the human cultivation

What kinds of punishments will the evil spirits receive, who will have lost all power and authority, in the Abyss?

Before we move on further, keep in mind that evil spirits

174

only serve and exist only as instruments for the human cultivation. Why, then, does God cultivate human beings on the earth even though there are countless heavenly host and angels in Heaven? That is because God wants true children with whom He can share His love.

Let me give you an example. Throughout the history of Korea, the nobility usually had many servants in their households. Servants would obey whatever their master commanded. Now, a master has prodigal sons and daughters who do not obey him but only do whatever they please. Does this mean the master will love his obedient servants more than his prodigal children? He cannot help loving his children even though they may not be the most obedient.

It is the same with God. He loves human beings made in His image no matter how many obedient heavenly host and angels He has. Heavenly host and angels are more like robots that only do what they are told. Thus, they are incapable of sharing true love with God.

Of course, it is not to say that angels and robots are the same in all aspects. On the one hand, robots do only as they are commanded, lack free will, and cannot feel anything. On the other hand, like human beings angels know the feeling of joy and sorrow.

When you feel joy or sorrow, angels do not have the same feeling you have, but merely know what it is that you are feeling. Therefore, when you praise God, angels will praise Him with you. When you dance to glorify God, they will also dance and even play musical instruments together. This trait distinguishes them from robots. Yet, angels and robots are "alike" in that they both lack free will and do only as they are told, made and used only as tools or instruments.

Like the angels, the evil spirits are nothing but tools used for the human cultivation. They are like machines that do not distinguish the good from the evil, made for a certain purpose, and they are used for an evil purpose.

The evil spirits confined in the Abyss

The law of the spiritual world dictates that "the wages of sin is death" and "A man reaps what he sows." After the Great Judgment, the souls in the Lower Grave will suffer from the lake of fire or burning sulfur according to this law. It is because they chose evil in their free will and feelings while they were being cultivated on the earth.

The evil spirits except for the demons are not relevant to the human cultivation. Thus, even after the Judgment, the evil spirits are confined in the dark and cold Abyss, abandoned like a pile of rubbish. This is the most suitable punishment for them.

God's Throne is located in the center and the apex of Heaven. Conversely, the evil spirits are locked in the Abyss, the deepest and darkest place in Hell. They cannot move around comfortably in the dark and cold Abyss. As if they are pressed down by huge rocks, the evil spirits will forever be confined in a fixed position.

These evil spirits had once belonged to Heaven and had glorious duties. After their fall, the fallen angels used authority in their own way in the world of darkness. However, they were defeated in a war they had waged on God and all was over. They lost all the glory and value as heavenly beings. In the Abyss, as a symbol of curse and disgrace, the wings of these fallen angels will have been ripped apart.

A spirit is an eternal being and immortal. Yet, an evil spirit in the Abyss cannot even move a finger, has no feeling, will, or power. They are like machines that have been switched off, or dolls that have been thrown out, and even appear to be frozen.

Some messengers of hell remain in the Lower Grave

There is an exception to this rule. As mentioned above, children under the age of roughly twelve will remain in the Lower Grave even after the Judgment. Thus, in order for punishments of these children to continue, the messengers of hell to administer are necessary.

These messengers of hell are not confined in the Abyss but remain in the Lower Grave. They look like robots. Before the Judgment, they would sometimes laugh and enjoy the sight of souls being tortured, but that was not because they themselves had any emotions. It was the control of Lucifer, who had human characteristics, who drove the messengers of hell to display emotions. After the Judgment, however, they are no longer controlled by Lucifer, but they will do their work without any feelings, working like machines.

Where Will the Demons End Up?

Unlike fallen angels, dragons and their followers that had been created before the creation of the universe, demons are not spiritual beings. They were once human beings, made from the dust, and had spirits, souls, and bodies like us. Among those once cultivated in this world but died without receiving salvation are those released to this world under special

177

circumstances as demons.

How, then, does one become a demon? There are usually four ways through which people become demons.

The first is the case of people who have sold their spirits and souls to Satan.

People who practice sorcery and seek help and power from the evil spirits to satisfy their greed and desire, such as the sorcerers, can become demons when they die.

The second is the case of people who have committed suicide in their own evil.

If people ended their lives on their own because of the failure of business or other reasons, they have ignored God's sovereignty over life and can become demons. However, this is not the same as to sacrifice one's life for his/her country or help the helpless. If a man, who himself did not know how to swim, had jumped into the water to rescue someone else at the expense of his own life, it was for a good and noble purpose.

The third is the case of people who had once believed in God but ended up denying Him and selling their faith.

Some believers reproach and oppose God when faced with great difficulties or lose someone or something very dear to them. Charles Darwin, the pioneer of the theory of evolution, is a good example. Darwin had once believed in God the Creator. When his beloved daughter died prematurely, Darwin came to deny and oppose God and launched the theory of evolution. Such people commit the sin of crucifying Jesus Christ, our Redeemer, all over again (Hebrews 6:6).

The fourth and last is the case of people who obstruct, oppose, and blaspheme the Holy Spirit even though they believe in God and know the truth (Matthew 12:31-32; Luke 12:10).

Today, many people who apparently profess their belief in God obstruct, oppose, and blaspheme the Holy Spirit. Even as these people witness countless works of God, they nevertheless judge and condemn others, oppose the works of the Holy Spirit, and try to destroy churches accompanied with His works. Besides, if they do so as leaders, their sins become all the more severe.

When these sinners die, they are thrown into the Lower Grave and receive the third or fourth level of punishments. The fact is that some of these souls become demons and are released to this world.

Demons controlled by the devil

Until the Judgment, Lucifer has the complete authority to control the world of darkness and the Lower Grave. Thus, Lucifer also has power to select certain souls most suitable for her works from the Lower Grave and use them in this world as demons.

Once these souls are selected and released to the world, unlike they had during their lifetime, they no longer have the will or feelings of their own. According to Lucifer's will, they are controlled by the devil and serve only as the instruments to fulfill goals of the world of evil spirits.

The demons tempt people on the earth to love the world. Some of today's most atrocious sins and crimes are not a coincidence but made possible through the work of demons according to the will of Lucifer. Demons enter those people according to the law of the spiritual world and lead them to Hell. Sometimes, demons make people crippled and bring them diseases. Of course, this does not mean that every kind and case of deformity or illness is attributed to demons but some cases are brought upon by demons. We find in the Bible a demon-possessed boy who had been mute since childhood (Mark 9:17-24), and a woman who had been crippled by a spirit for eighteen years was bent over, and could not straighten herself up (Luke 13:10-13).

According to the will of Lucifer, demons have been assigned the lightest of duties in the world of darkness but they will not be confined in the Abyss after the Judgment. Since the demons had once been human beings and cultivated, along with those who received the third or fourth levels of punishments in the Lower Grave, they will be thrown into the lake of burning sulfur after the Judgment of the Great White Throne.

Evil spirits are frightened of the Abyss

Some of you who remember the words in the Bible may find something to be amiss. In Luke 8, there is a scene in which Jesus meets with a demon-possessed man. When He commanded the demon to come out of the man, the demon said, *"What business do we have with each other, Jesus, Son of the Most High God? I beg You, do not torment me!"* (Luke 8:28) and pleaded with Jesus so that He would not send it into the Abyss.

Demons are destined to be thrown into the lake of burning sulfur, not the Abyss. Why, then, did it ask Jesus not to send it to the Abyss? As mentioned above, demons had once been human beings and as such, they are mere instruments used for the human cultivation according to the will of Lucifer. Thus, when the demon spoke to Jesus through the lips of this man, it was expressing the heart of the evil spirits who control it, not of its own. The evil spirits headed by Lucifer know that once God's providence of the human cultivation is complete, they will lose all their authorities and power and will be eternally confined in the Abyss. Their fear for the future all too clear was shown through the demon's pleading.

Furthermore, the demon was used as an instrument so that these evil spirits' fear as well as their end could be recorded in the Bible.

Why do demons loathe North Korea, water, and fire?

Early in my ministry, the Holy Spirit worked so powerfully in my church that the blind came to see, the mute came to speak, people with polios came to walk, and the evil spirits were driven out. This news spread throughout the country, and many sick people came. At that time, I personally prayed for the demon-possessed, and the demons, as spiritual beings knew in advance that they would be driven away. At times, some demons would beg me, "Please do not drive us out to water, fire, or North Korea!"

Of course, I could not agree to their requests. After that, I prayed, "God, why do demons loathe North Korea?" In response, God revealed to me that demons hate North Korea because people in the isolated country cannot and do not worship idols and thus will not accept demons.

Why, then, do demons hate water and fire? The Bible has recorded their resentment against water and fire as well. When I prayed again for revelation on this, God told me that spiritually water stands for life, more specifically the Word of God who is the light itself. Moreover, fire symbolizes the fire of the Holy Spirit. Accordingly, demons that represent the darkness itself will lose their power and authority when they are driven out into fire or water.

In Mark 5 is a scene in which Jesus commands the demon "Legion" to come out of a man, and they begged Him to send them among the pigs (Mark 5:12). Jesus gave them permission, and the evil spirits came out of the man and went into the pigs. The herd of pigs, about two thousands in number, rushed down the steep bank into the lake and were drowned. Jesus did this to prevent these demons from working for Lucifer any further by drowning them in a lake. This does not mean, however, that the demons were drowned; they only lost their power. That is why Jesus tells us that *"when the unclean spirit goes out of a man, it passes through waterless places seeking rest, and does not find it"* (Matthew 12:43).

The children of God should know the spiritual world clearly in order to display God's power. Demons tremble in fear if you drive them out with the full knowledge of the spiritual world. Yet, they will not tremble, much less be driven out, if you just utter "You demon, get out and go into the water! Go into the fire!" without having the spiritual understanding.

Lucifer struggles to establish her kingdom

God is the God of abundant love but He is also the God of justice. No matter how merciful and forgiving any kings of this world may be, they cannot be merciful and forgiving unconditionally at all times. When there are thieves and murderers in the country, a king should catch and punish them according to the law of the land in order to maintain peace and security for his people. Even when his beloved son or people commit serious crimes such as treason, the king has no other option but punish them according to the law.

Likewise, the love of God is the kind of love that is in line with the strict order of the spiritual world. God had greatly loved Lucifer before her betrayal, and even after the betrayal, God gave Lucifer a complete authority over the darkness, but the only reward Lucifer will receive is the confinement in the Abyss. Since Lucifer already knows this fact, she is struggling to establish her kingdom and keep it stand firm. For this reason, Lucifer killed many prophets of God two thousand years ago and before then. Two thousand years ago, when Lucifer found out about the birth of Jesus, in order to prevent the kingdom of God from being established and to perpetually maintain her kingdom of darkness, she tried to kill Jesus through King Herod. After having been instigated by Satan, Herod gave orders to kill all the boys in the land who were two years old and under (Matthew 2:13-18).

Besides this, during the last two millennia, Lucifer has always tried to destroy and kill anyone who displayed the wondrous power of God. Yet, Lucifer can never prevail against God or surpass His wisdom, and her end is found only in the Abyss.

God of love waits and gives opportunities for repentance

All people on the earth are bound to be judged according to their deeds. For the unjust wait curses and punishments and for the good wait blessings and glory. However, God who Himself is love does not immediately throw people who have just sinned into Hell. He waits patiently for people to repent as recorded in 2 Peter 3:8-9, *"But do not let this one fact escape your notice, beloved, that with the Lord one day is like a thousand years, and a thousand years like one day. The Lord is not slow about His promise, as some count slowness, but is patient toward you, not wishing for any to perish but for all to come to repentance."* This is the love of God who wants all people to receive salvation.

Through this message on Hell, you should remember that God was also patient and waited for all those being punished in the Lower Grave. This God of love laments for the souls, created in His image and His likeness, who are now suffering and will be suffering for ages to come.

Despite God's patience and love, if people do not accept the gospel to the end or claim to believe but keep on sinning, they will lose all the opportunities for salvation and fall into Hell.

This is why we believers should always be spreading the gospel whether or not we have an opportunity. Let us suppose that there was a big fire at your house while you were out. When you came back, the house was engulfed in flames and your children were sleeping inside. Will you not do all you can to rescue your children? God's heart is all the more broken when He sees people who are created in His image and His likeness commit sins and fall into the eternal flames of Hell. Similarly, can you imagine how delighted God would be to see people leading other people to salvation?

You should understand the heart of God that loves all people and mourns for those who are on the way to Hell, as well as the heart of Jesus Christ who does not want to lose even one person. Now that you have read about the cruelty and misery of Hell, you may be able to understand why God is so pleased with the salvation of people. I hope that you will grasp and feel the heart of God so that you will spread the good news and lead people to Heaven.

Chapter 9

Why Did the God of Love Have to Prepare Hell?

About two thousand years ago, Jesus went throughout the towns and villages in Israel, preached the good news and healed every disease. When He encountered people, Jesus had compassion on them, because they were harassed and helpless, like sheep without a shepherd (Matthew 9:36). There were countless people who were to be saved, but there was no one to look after them. Even if Jesus diligently went around the villages and visited people, He could not take care of all of them one by one.

In Matthew 9:37-38, Jesus told His disciples, *"The harvest is plentiful, but the workers are few. Therefore beseech the Lord of the harvest to send out workers into His harvest."* Very much needed were the workers who would teach countless people the truth with burning love and drive away the darkness from them in Jesus' place.

Nowadays, so many people are enslaved by sin, suffering from disease, poverty, and grief, and are heading towards Hell – all because they do not know the truth. We have to understand the heart of Jesus who is seeking workers to send into the harvest field, so that you will not only receive salvation but also confess to Him, "Here I am! Send me, Lord."

God's Patience and Love

There was a son who was loved and adored by his parents. One day, this son asked his parents to give him his share of the estate. They complied with the son's request, even though they could not quite understand their son, to whom they were going to bequeath everything anyway. Then the son went abroad with his share of the estate. Even though he had hopes and ambitions in the beginning, he increasingly gave into pleasure and passion of the world and wasted all his wealth in the end. Moreover, the country faced a severe depression so he became even poorer. One day, someone delivered the news about the son to his parents, telling them that their son became as good as a beggar due to a life of dissipation, and was thus despised by people.

What must his parents have felt? They might have been angry first, but soon they would begin worrying about him, thinking, 'We forgive you, son. Just come back home quickly!'

God accepts children who return in repentance

The heart of these parents is recorded in Luke 15. The father, whose son had set off for a distant country, waited for his son at the gate everyday. The father was waiting for the return of his son so desperately that when his son did return, the father could immediately recognize him even from a distance, ran to his son, and threw his arms around him joyfully. The father put on the repenting son the best robe and sandals, killed the fattened calf, and held a feast in the son's honor.

This is the heart of God. He not only forgives all those who earnestly repent, regardless of the amount or severity of their sins, but also comforts and empowers them to do better. When one person is saved by faith, God rejoices and celebrates the occasion with the heavenly host and angels. Our merciful God is love itself. With the heart of the father waiting for his son, God eagerly wants all people to turn from sin and receive salvation.

The God of love and forgiveness

Through Hosea chapter 3, you can get a glimpse of the abundant mercy and compassion of our God, who is always eager to forgive and love even sinners.

One day, God ordered Hosea to take an adulterous woman as his wife. Hosea obeyed and married Gomer. A few years later, however, Gomer was unable to keep her heart and loved another man. Furthermore, she was paid like a prostitute and went to love another man. God then told Hosea, *"Go again, love a woman who is loved by her husband, yet an adulteress, even as the LORD loves the sons of Israel, though they turn to other gods and love raisin cakes"* (v. 1). God ordered Hosea to love his wife, who had betrayed him and left home to love another man. Hosea brought Gomer back after paying for fifteen shekels of silver and a homer and a half of barley (v. 2). How many people can do that? After Hosea brought Gomer back, he told her, *"You shall stay with me for many days. You shall not play the harlot, nor shall you have a man; so I will also be toward you"* (v. 3). He did not condemn or hate her, but forgave her with love and pleaded with her never to leave him again.

What Hosea did seems foolish in the sight of the people of this world. However, his heart symbolizes God's heart. The way

Hosea married an adulterous woman, God first loved us, who had left Him, and even delivered us.

After Adam's disobedience, all human beings were imbued with sin. Like Gomer, they were not worthy of God's love. However, God nevertheless loved them and gave them His one and only Son Jesus to be crucified. This Jesus was whipped, wore a crown of thorns, and was nailed on His hands and feet so that He could save us. Even as He was hanging on the cross dying, He prayed, "Father, forgive them." Even as we speak, Jesus is interceding for all sinners before the Throne of our God the Father in Heaven.

Yet, so many people do not know God's love and grace. Instead, they love the world and keep on sinning in pursuant of their desires of flesh. Some live in the darkness because they do not know the truth. Others know the truth but as time goes by, their hearts change and they commit sins again. Once they are saved, people have to sanctify themselves daily. However, their hearts become corrupt and contaminated unlike the time when they first received the Holy Spirit. That is why these people even commit the kind of evil they had once cast off before.

God still wants to forgive and love even the people who have sinned and loved the world. Just as Hosea brought back his adulterous wife who loved another man, God is waiting for the return and repentance of His children who have sinned.

Therefore, we have to understand the heart of God who has revealed to us the message on Hell. God does not want to frighten us; He only wants us to learn about the misery of Hell, thoroughly repent, and receive salvation. The message on Hell is a way for Him to express His burning love for us. We must also understand why God had to prepare Hell so that we can understand His heart more deeply and spread the good news to more people to save them from eternal punishments.

Why Did the God of Love Have to Prepare Hell?

Genesis 2:7 reads, *"Then the LORD God formed man of dust from the ground, and breathed into his nostrils the breath of life; and man became a living being."*

In 1983, the year after the doors to my church opened, God showed me a vision in which the creation of Adam was depicted. God was happily and joyously molding Adam from the clay with care and love, as if a child were playing with his/ her most favorite toy or doll. After delicately molding Adam, God breathed into his nostrils the breath of life. Because we received the breath of life from God, who is Spirit, our spirit and soul are immortal. Flesh made from the dust will perish and return to a handful of dust, but our spirit and soul last forever.

For that reason, God had to prepare for places for these immortal spirits to dwell, and they are Heaven and Hell. As recorded in 2 Peter 2:9-10, people who live God-fearing lives will be saved and enter Heaven, but the unrighteous will be punished in Hell.

Then the Lord knows how to rescue the godly from temptation, and to keep the unrighteous under punishment for the day of judgment, and especially those who indulge the flesh in its corrupt desires and despise authority. Daring, self-willed, they do not tremble when they revile angelic majesties.

191

On the one hand, God's children will live under His eternal reign in Heaven. Thus, Heaven is always full of happiness and joy. On the other hand, Hell is a place for all those who did not accept God's love but instead betrayed Him and became a slave to sin. In Hell, they will receive cruel punishments. Why, then, did the God of love have to prepare Hell?

God separates the wheat from the chaff

As a farmer sows seeds and cultivates them, God cultivates human beings in this world to gain true children. When the time for the harvest comes, He separates the wheat from the chaff, sending the wheat to Heaven and the chaff to Hell.

His winnowing fork is in His hand, and He will thoroughly clear His threshing floor; and He will gather His wheat into the barn, but He will burn up the chaff with unquenchable fire (Matthew 3:12).

The "wheat" here symbolizes all those who accept Jesus Christ, try to recover God's image, and live according to His Word. The "chaff" refers to those who do not accept Jesus Christ as their Savior, but love the world, and follow evil.

As a farmer gathers the wheat into a barn and burns the chaff or uses it as fertilizer in harvest, God also brings the wheat into Heaven and throws the chaff into Hell.

God wants to make sure that we know about the existence of the Lower Grave and Hell. Lava under the surface of the earth and fire serve as a reminder of eternal punishments in Hell. If there were no fire or sulfur in this world, how could we have even imagined the ghastly scenes of the Lower Grave and

Hell? God created these things because they are necessary for the cultivation of human beings.

The reason "the chaff" are thrown into the fire of Hell

Some may ask, "Why did the God of love prepare Hell? Why can't He let the chaff into Heaven, too?"

The beauty of Heaven is beyond any imagination or description. God, the master of Heaven is holy without any blemish or flaw and thus, only those who do His will are allowed to enter Heaven (Matthew 7:21). If wicked people were in Heaven along with people full of love and goodness, life in Heaven will be extremely difficult and awkward, and the beautiful Heaven will only be contaminated. This is why God had to prepare Hell to separate the wheat in Heaven from the chaff in Hell.

Without Hell, the righteous and the wicked will be forced to live together. Should that have been the case, Heaven will become a haven of darkness, filled with shrieking and cries in agony. However, the purpose of God's human cultivation is not to create such a place. Heaven is a place without tears, sorrow, torment, and disease, where He can share His abundant love with His children forever more. Thus, Hell is necessary to perpetually confine the wicked and worthless people – the chaff.

Romans 6:16 reads, *"Do you not know that when you present yourselves to someone as slaves for obedience, you are slaves of the one whom you obey, either of sin resulting in death, or of obedience resulting in righteousness?"* Even if they may not have known it, all those who do not live according to God's Word are slaves to sin and slaves to our enemy Satan and the devil. On this earth, they are controlled by the enemy Satan and the devil; after death, they will be thrown into the hands of those evil spirits in Hell and receive all sorts of punishments.

God rewards everyone according to what he/she had done

Our God is not only the God of love, mercy, and kindness but also a fair and just God who rewards each of us according to our deeds. Galatians 6:7-8 reads:

Do not be deceived, God is not mocked; for whatever a man sows, this he will also reap. For the one who sows to his own flesh will from the flesh reap corruption, but the one who sows to the Spirit will from the Spirit reap eternal life.

On the one hand, when you sow prayers and praises, you will be empowered to live according to the Word of God with power from Heaven, and your spirit and soul will be made well. When you sow with faithful services, all your parts – spirit, soul, and body – will be strengthened. When you sow money through the tithe or thanksgiving offerings, you will be financially blessed more abundantly so that you can sow more for God's kingdom and righteousness. On the other hand, when you sow evil, you will be paid back the exact amount and magnitude of your evil. Even if you are a believer, when you sow sins and lawlessness, you will face trials. Therefore, I hope that you will be enlightened and learn this fact with the help of the Holy Spirit, so that you may receive eternal life.

In John 5:28-29, Jesus told us that *"Do not marvel at this;*

for an hour is coming, in which all who are in the tombs will hear His voice, and will come forth; those who did the good deeds to a resurrection of life, those who committed the evil deeds to a resurrection of judgment." In Matthew 16:27, Jesus promised us, *"For the Son of Man is going to come in the glory of His Father with His angels, and will then repay every man according to his deeds."*

With impeccable accuracy, through the Judgment God rewards appropriate prizes and allocate appropriate punishments to everyone according to what he/she has done. Whether each individual will go to Heaven or Hell is not up to God but up to each individual who has the free will, and everyone will reap what he/she sows.

God Wants All People to Receive Salvation

God deems a person created in His image and likeness more important than the entire universe. Thus, God wants all men to believe in Jesus Christ and receive salvation.

God rejoices even more when one sinner repents

With the heart of the shepherd who searches around rugged roads for one lost sheep even though he has another ninety-nine sheep secured (Luke 15:4-7), God rejoices all the more over one sinner who repents than ninety-nine righteous people who do not need to repent.

The Psalmist wrote in Psalm 103:121-3, *"As far as the east is from the west, so far has He removed our transgressions from us. Just as a father has compassion on his children, so the LORD has compassion on those who fear Him."* God also promised in Isaiah 1:18 that *"Come now, and let us reason together. Though your sins are as scarlet, they will be as white as snow; though they are red like crimson, they will be like wool."*

God is the Light itself and in Him, there is no darkness. He is also the goodness itself, who loathes sin, but when a sinner comes before Him and repents, God does not remember his sins. Instead, God embraces and blesses the sinner in His unlimited forgiveness and warm love.

If you understand God's amazing love even a little, you ought to treat each individual with earnest love. You should have compassion on those who are going towards the fire of Hell, pray earnestly for them, share the good news with them, and visit those who have weak faith and strengthen their faith so that they may stand firm.

If you do not repent

1 Timothy 2:4 tells us, *"[God] desires all men to be saved and to come to the knowledge of the truth."* God desperately wants all people to know Him, receive salvation, and come to where He is. God is anxious for the salvation of even one more person, waiting for the people in the darkness and sin to turn to Him.

However, even if God has given people countless opportunities to repent, to the extent of sacrificing His only Son on the cross, if they do not repent and die, only one fact remains for them. According to the law of the spiritual world, they will reap what they sow and be paid back according to what they have done, and thrown into Hell in the end.

I hope that you will realize this amazing love and justice

of God so that you may receive Jesus Christ and be forgiven. Moreover, behave and live according to the will of God so that you may shine like the sun in Heaven.

Boldly Spread the Gospel

Those who know and truly believe in the existence of Heaven and Hell cannot help evangelizing, because they know the heart of God who wants all men to receive salvation all too well.

Without people to spread the good news

Romans 10:14-15 tells us that God praises those who spread the good news:

How then will they call on Him in whom they have not believed? How will they believe in Him whom they have not heard? And how will they hear without a preacher? How will they preach unless they are sent? Just as it is written, "How beautiful are the feet of those who bring good news of good things!"

In 2 Kings 5, there is a story about Naaman, a commander of the army of the king of Aram. Naaman was considered a high and noble man by his king because he had saved his country many times. He gained fame and wealth, and lacked nothing. Yet, Naaman had leprosy. In those days, leprosy was an incurable disease and considered as the curse from Heaven, so Naaman's valor and riches were now useless to him. Even his own king could not help him.

Can you imagine the heart of Naaman who was watching his once-healthy body rotting and decaying day by day? Furthermore, even the members of his own family kept distance from Naaman, fearing that they, too, might become infected with the disease. How powerless and helpless must Naaman have felt?

Yet, God had a good plan for Naaman, a gentile commander. There was a maidservant who had been captured in Israel, now serving Naaman's wife.

Naaman is healed after listening to his maidservant

The maidservant, though she was a little girl, knew the way to resolve Naaman's problem. The girl believed that Elisha, a prophet in Samaria, could heal her master's disease. She boldly delivered the news about God's power displayed through Elisha to her master. She did not keep her mouth shut especially about something in which she had a great deal of faith. After hearing this news, Naaman prepared offerings with his utmost sincerity and went to see the prophet.

What do you think happened to Naaman? He was completely healed by the power of God who was with Elisha. He even confessed, *"Behold now, I know that there is no God in all the earth, but in Israel"* (2 Kings 5:15). Naaman was cured not only of his illness, but the problem of his spirit was also resolved.

On this story, Jesus comments in Luke 4:27: *"And there were many lepers in Israel in the time of Elisha the prophet; and none of them was cleansed, but only Naaman the Syrian."* Why could only Naaman the gentile be healed even though there were many other lepers in Israel? That is because Naaman's heart was genuinely good and humble enough to listen to other people's advices. Even though Naaman was a gentile, God prepared the way of salvation for him because he was a good man, always a faithful general to his king, and a servant who loved his people so much that he could and would willingly lay down his life for them.

However, if the maidservant had not delivered the message of the power of Elisha to Naaman, he would have died without being healed, much less receiving salvation. The life of a noble and worthy warrior depended upon the lips of a little girl.

Boldly preach the gospel

As was the case with Naaman, many people around you are waiting for you to open your mouth. Even in this life, they are suffering from many difficulties of life and advancing towards Hell every day. How pitiful will it be if they are to be eternally tormented after such a difficult life on the earth? Therefore, God's children must boldly deliver the gospel to such people.

God will be immensely delighted when, through the power of the Lord, people who were to die receive life, and people who were suffering become free. He will also make them prosper and healthy, telling them, "You are my child who refreshes my spirit." Moreover, God will help them gain faith great enough to enter the glorious city of New Jerusalem, where the Throne of God is located. Besides, would not the very people who heard the good news and accepted Jesus Christ through you be also grateful for what you have done for them?

If people during this life do not possess faith great enough to be saved, they will never have "a second chance" once they go to Hell. In the midst of eternal suffering and agony, they can only regret and lament forever and ever.

For you to have heard the gospel and accepted the Lord, there were immeasurable sacrifice and dedication of countless forefathers of faith, who had been killed with swords, fallen to prey of hungry ferocious beasts, or embraced martyrdom for proclaiming the good news.

What should you do, then, now that you know you have been saved from Hell? You must try your best to deliver many souls from Hell to the arms of the Lord. In 1 Corinthians 9:16, the apostle Paul confessed his mission with a burning heart: *"For if I preach the gospel, I have nothing to boast of, for I am under compulsion; for woe is me if I do not preach the gospel."*

I hope you will go into the world with a burning heart of the Lord and save many souls from the eternal punishment of Hell.

You have known about the eternal, ghastly, and wretched place called Hell through this book. I pray that you will feel the love of God, who does not want to lose even one person, keep alert in your own Christian life, and deliver the gospel to anyone who needs to hear it.

In God's eyes, you are more precious than the entire world and worthier than everything in the universe combined, because you were created in His own image. Therefore, you must not become a slave to sin who opposes God and end up in Hell, but become a true child of God who walks in the light, acts and lives according to the truth.

With the same degree of delight God had when He created

Adam, He is watching over you even today. He wants you to achieve the true heart, mature in faith swiftly, and attain to the whole measure of the fullness of Christ.

In the name of the Lord, I pray that you will promptly accept Jesus Christ and receive the blessings and authority as a precious child of God, so that you may play the role of salt and light in the world, and lead countless people to salvation!

The Author
Dr. Jaerock Lee

Dr. Jaerock Lee was born in Muan, Jeonnam Province, Republic of Korea, in 1943. In his twenties, he suffered from a variety of incurable diseases for seven years and awaited death with no hope for recovery. One day in the spring of 1974, however, he was led to a church by his sister, and when he knelt down to pray, the living God immediately healed him of all his diseases.

From the moment Dr. Lee met the living God through that wonderful experience, he has loved God with all his heart and sincerity, and in 1978 was called to be a servant of God. He prayed fervently so that he could clearly understand the will of God and wholly accomplish it, and obeyed all the Word of God. In 1982, he founded Manmin Church in Seoul, S. Korea, and countless works of God, including miraculous healings and wonders, have been taking place at his church.

In 1986, Dr. Lee was ordained as a pastor at the Annual Assembly of Jesus' Sungkyul Church of Korea, and four years later in 1990, his sermons began to be broadcast on the Far East Broadcasting Company, the Asia Broadcast Station, and the Washington Christian Radio System to Australia, Russia, the Philippines, and many more.

Three years later in 1993, Manmin Central Church was selected as one of the "World's Top 50 Churches" by the *Christian World* magazine (US) and he received an Honorary Doctorate of Divinity from Christian Faith College, Florida, USA, and in 1996 a Ph. D. in Ministry from Kingsway Theological Seminary, Iowa, USA.

Since 1993, Dr. Lee has taken the lead in world mission through many overseas crusades in Israel, L.A., New York, Baltimore, Hawaii of the USA,

Tanzania, Argentina, Uganda, Japan, Pakistan, Kenya, the Philippines, Honduras, India, Russia, Germany, Peru, and Democratic Republic of Congo, and in 2002 he was called a "worldwide pastor" by major Christian newspapers in Korea for his work in various overseas crusades.

As of September 2010, Manmin Central Church is a congregation of more than 100,000 members and has 9,000 branch churches throughout the globe including 53 domestic branch churches in major cities, and has so far commissioned more than 132 missionaries to 23 countries, including the United States, Russia, Germany, Canada, Japan, China, France, India, Kenya, and many more.

To this day, Dr. Lee has written 60 books, including bestsellers *Tasting Eternal Life before Death, My Life My Faith I & II, The Message of the Cross, The Measure of Faith, Heaven I & II,* and *Hell,* and his works have been being translated into more than 47 languages.

His Christian columns appear on *The Hankook Ilbo, The JoongAng Daily, The Dong-A Ilbo, The Munhwa Ilbo, The Seoul Shinmun, The Kyunghyang Shinmun, The Hankyoreh Shinmun, The Korea Economic Daily, The Korea Herald, The Shisa News, The Christian Press.*

Dr. Lee is currently leader of many missionary organizations and associations including: Chairman, The United Holiness Church of Jesus Christ; Permanent President of the World Christianity Revival Mission Association; President, Manmin World Mission; Founder, Manmin TV; Founder & Board Chairman, Global Christian Network (GCN); Founder & Board Chairman, World Christian Doctors Network (WCDN); and Founder & Board Chairman, Manmin International Seminary (MIS).

Heaven I & II

A detailed sketch of the gorgeous living environment the heavenly citizens enjoy and beautiful description of different levels of heavenly kingdoms.

The Message of the Cross

A powerful awakening message for all the people who are spiritually asleep In this book you will find the reason Jesus is the only Savior and the true love of God.

The Measure of Faith

What kind of a dwelling place, crown and reward are prepared for you in Heaven? This book provides with wisdom and guidance for you to measure your faith and cultivate the best and most mature faith.

Tasting Eternal Life Before Death

A testimonial memoirs of Dr. Jaerock Lee, who was born again and saved from the valley of death and has been leading an exemplary Christian life.

Awaken, Israel

Why has God kept His eyes on Israel from the beginning of the world to this day? What kind of His providence has been prepared for Israel in the last days, who await the Messiah?